Smelling the Taste of Sound

A professional woman's story of a late autism diagnosis

The Autistic Lawyer

Synaesthesia Publishing

For B, who loves me for me and lets me be me

Disclaimer

Please note that details and specifics shared in this book concerning: names, roles, positions, staff, colleagues, clients, cases, places, locations, descriptions, diagnoses, conditions, offences, dates, quotes, dialogue, statements and anecdotes have been altered to respect privacy and ensure anonymity.

I have also drawn upon different times and experiences in my life to exemplify points raised, which will assist in a greater understanding of neurodiversity through illustration. Any resemblance to persons, living or dead, or events, is purely coincidental due to changes being made.

This book cannot be used to obtain or provide legal advice in any jurisdiction. Furthermore, I am not a doctor, clinician, or any kind of healthcare professional. This book cannot be used to diagnose any conditions or disorders, developmental or otherwise. I write solely from my perspective, views and experience. This is because I think that I may be able to help neurodivergent people who want to learn more about neurodiversity, people who spend time with those who are neurodivergent, and those who know nothing at all and would like to know a bit more.

I write anonymously because it gives me more freedom to express my views and opinions as well as share my experiences. That said, my name is unimportant. What is important, is that if you're autistic, this doesn't mean that you can't achieve your dreams and ambitions. The name I use is about what one *can* achieve.

My dream was to be a lawyer. Now my dream is to promote greater fairness and equality around autism and other types of neurodivergence.

I want the world to be a better, kinder and more understanding place for those of us who are wired differently. This will only come from a greater appreciation and willingness to change. I shall keep talking until I succeed.

The Autistic Lawyer

October 2023

Contents

Preface

I decided to write this book because, in my experience, people's understanding of neurodiversity and its manifestations is woefully inadequate. Because of this, society (and especially the workplace) is missing out. Neurodivergent people have much to offer an employer and I want our voices to be heard.

I *especially* want the voices of autistic females to ring out loud and clear because autism has been seen as a male condition for too long. My autism wouldn't have been 'picked up' years ago, but now we're seeing so many more people (especially women and famous ones at that) receiving a diagnosis. I think this is probably due to an increase in awareness and more refined diagnostic criteria.

Opinions differ when it comes to the prevalence of autism. However, about one in one hundred people (1%) are believed to be autistic, so that's around 700,000 of us here in the UK. I think the figure is much higher, especially due to the underdiagnosing of females.

The workplace can be daunting for many people, but it's often an incredibly stressful environment for neurodivergent people, and given that we spend huge chunks of our lives at work, it needs to be made more autism friendly.

Furthermore, in the UK in 2021, only 29% of autistic adults were employed. Admittedly, some are unlikely ever to be able to enter the workplace, but I think a lot more could and would like to; they may just need a few small changes to be made. This group of people has a lot to offer, so as a society, we need to raise our game.

I am not an authority on neurodiversity. I'm merely drawing on my own experience and understanding of autism and other types of neurodivergence to help people and raise awareness.

Throughout this book, I'll share with you my understanding of my neurodivergence through the female prism of a 'later-in-life' diagnosis and how so many things suddenly made sense, especially around why I was like I was as a child and why I struggled with what many would consider simple tasks, situations and circumstances. I've shared my experiences so I can provide first-hand what I've encountered and how things could be better for people, *especially* women like me.

Shortly after I'd received my diagnoses and while still learning about my conditions, I found myself working in a new career with clients, some of whom were neurodivergent themselves. So, I had to learn quickly, not just how to best manage the 'new me' but how to best serve a diverse and challenging client group.

Professionally, I dealt with people accused of serious criminal offences, people who'd been in prison for decades, people with profound mental health conditions and others who were facing the prospect of having their children removed from their care, to name but a few of the areas in which I worked.

At the same time, I was trying to understand my 'new' diagnoses. The office environment was unconventional and not what one may expect of a law firm. Some of the stories are tragic, some are hilarious and most were like nothing I had encountered before. We were seeing people at some of the lowest points in their lives, so we got to see the very worst and the very best of human nature.

I'll share with you how I got to grips with retraining later in life in a thought-provoking environment while still trying to understand neurodiversity. I encountered clients from a world many don't get to see and I blend these two distinct narratives.

Introduction

At age thirty, I decided to pursue a career in law. I left my job in the corporate world to retrain as a solicitor. Three years later, I was diagnosed with several conditions, including autism and Attention Deficit Hyperactivity Disorder (ADHD). Shortly after being diagnosed, I joined a tough, gritty law firm as a trainee solicitor, where much of the work was publicly funded.

Starting a new job and career in your thirties would be challenging for most people. However, when you've just received diagnoses that you're still learning about and trying to fathom how best to get along with these 'new' facets in your life, the experience is not to be underestimated.

These 'newcomers' had always been part of me and my persona but had previously gone undetected while hiding in plain sight. Little did I know that my newcomers would be the most straightforward aspect of my newly acquired life.

I had joined a working environment that would have tested the mettle of the steeliest hard case. Not only was there poverty and deprivation but the breadth and depth of legal assistance some clients required was incredible.

The firm helped many people, including those facing serious criminal charges, individuals with mental health issues, people with housing and employment problems, prisoners, and parents trying to have their children returned to their care following local authority removal. These are just a few examples of the expertise and services undertaken, and I worked in a number of areas. Sometimes, clients would utilise many of the firm's departments simultaneously, such was the complexity of their needs.

As comical, enlightening and humbling as some of the cases were, nothing could have prepared me for the incendiary office environment, explosive characters and volatility on an almost daily basis and this was coming from some of the staff.

However, though the clients were a constant source of amusement, frustration and heartbreak, the person who was the day-to-day boss was incredibly unassuming and benign upon first meeting. Brenda had grafted her way up to manager and had made herself, family and friends cogs in many aspects of the firm's machinery, whether required or not.

This book covers some of my time at this firm and concludes when I qualified as a solicitor. Brenda was an essential part of this journey, but before I introduce her and the office in more depth, I'll first share with you a bit about my neurodivergence.

Chapter 1
A Smörgåsbord of Diagnoses

On 15 March 2017, I was diagnosed with autism, ADHD, dyslexia, dyscalculia and right-hemispheric deficit syndrome.

I was thirty-three, and it was a Wednesday.

For me, autistic thinking and neurotypical thinking are like two different operating systems used by different smartphone brands. Each functions very effectively, however, they are ostensibly quite different. More importantly, they aren't naturally compatible with one another without at least some kind of adaptation.

For years, autistic people just haven't had that adaptation. Society has not understood their format or been able to convert behaviours and characteristics into reasons and explanations for neurotypicals, the so-called 'normals', who are the majority and ruling class.

In my experience, having autism *and* ADHD is like having a wife *and* a mistress, although I'm not always sure which is which as they can be subject to change, rivalry and the odd spat.

At times, these developmental disabilities mitigate one another, and sometimes, they battle for primacy. ADHD gives me a relentless supply of energy, quick thinking and a flurry of ideas. However, this is soon tempered by the autism returning the much-needed order, logic, caution and structure to my thinking and behaviour. They are a bit of an odd couple, really, but they've been together for decades and have learned to rub along.

When my ADHD is in full flow and in need of a harness, I feel like a charioteer, battling the reins against the pull of my horses. Sometimes, I don't present as being particularly well-house-trained either, and it's a wonder anything comes out of my mouth with any semblance of order. My brain feels like an internet browser with thirty pages open all at once. I occasionally have little or no 'thought filter', and whatever is in my head tends to get propelled from my mouth with the rapidity of a bullet, although I'm getting better at auditing the content as I get older (assuming I can catch it)!

I always thought honesty was the best policy, but surprisingly, that's not true. 'Autistic honesty' and 'regular honesty' aren't necessarily the same thing because when somebody asks a question in search of an answer, it's not always honesty they're seeking. They might be looking for reassurance or support. Now, I'm not saying that I'm incapable of offering the latter; however, it's not my signature dish, so to speak.

When my autism is in the driving seat, I'm tense, intense, detail-obsessed, socially awkward and fraught with anxiety. In short, my ADHD is the accelerator, my autism is the brake and I'm a better motorist for hosting the two.

Increasing numbers of adults (especially women) and children are diagnosed as autistic. Whether this is because there is a genuine increase in numbers or whether it's because awareness has improved and professionals are just getting better at diagnosing, it's difficult to say.

In my opinion, it's the latter.

Those of us who are autistic haven't just materialised; we've been around for years. While diagnostic improvements are being made, girls, in particular, have often been overlooked. This is not because autism is a male condition or because girls aren't affected. I think it is because girls are more proficient at hiding their autism as well as presenting differently to boys. Professionals have largely worked from a male template, which I think accounts for many girls being missed.

I suspect this is why I wasn't picked up until I re-entered higher education years after leaving university. Initially, I thought I was just a little rusty as I'd been out of a learning environment for some time, coupled with knowing that numeracy had never been my strong suit. However, I became increasingly aware that I was struggling with some relatively straightforward tasks while managing others along with the rest of my contemporaries.

When I decided to study law, I completed a law conversion course designed for people who already held a degree, although not in law, but wanted to become a solicitor or barrister. It's a type of fast-track programme. The essential components of the law are condensed into this conversion course. Following the successful completion of this aspect of learning, one could then complete the Legal Practice Course (LPC) along with those who had studied law as an undergraduate to become a solicitor. This is where legal skills such as drafting documents, interviewing clients, working with accounts and undertaking tax calculations are taught.

During my LPC, I was advised that I might benefit from an assessment. So, I saw an educational psychologist. I'd never previously undergone any similar assessment. I was tested all day on many aspects of my intelligence, thinking and processing. When my results were shared with me, I had very mixed feelings.

As a child, I always felt very different from my peers. I hated going to parties and I didn't like group games or events. I didn't share in the interests of other children, be it in the latest doll or a cool new show on TV. This didn't bother me, as most of my peers just got on my nerves.

Getting my diagnosis was not like seeing a doctor and being provided with a solution, treatment, referral, prescription, or reassurance that there was nothing wrong. That's because if you present with a bacterial chest infection, you will be given an antibiotic, and you'll probably be referred for an investigation if you've found a lump. However, on the face of it, once you receive your neurodivergent diagnosis (whatever aspect of neurodiversity that may be), nothing happens, and nothing changes for the most part.

A diagnosis is just that. It's not a roadmap to explain how to manage your condition(s), and while you may now know that you're autistic or dyslexic, especially as an adult, what's changed? Several people asked me, "What will you do about it then?" Or they'd say, "What's next?" At first, I just shrugged my shoulders because I was just pleased and somewhat relieved to have some answers.

A diagnosis doesn't facilitate any 'solution', but a diagnosis did provide me with an opportunity to get to grips with coping strategies. Although, I think I was naïve when I thought everybody would be helpful and supportive. Some people were, but some certainly were not.

Once diagnosed, part of me felt relieved that I finally had an explanation as to why I was how I was, and the many things I didn't understand or I'd never heard of, I could go and read up on. But part of me felt saddened. I wondered what I might have achieved if I'd known earlier and coping strategies had been implemented. I'd never had extra time in exams or had people take time to explain things to me in an accessible or bespoke way, and that could have made things so much easier and less stressful for me. Instead, I'd just have to get on with it and rely upon my own coping strategies and determination to get where I wanted to be.

Having thought about this for some years, I believe I found out at the right time. I think having been diagnosed earlier with my 'smörgåsbord' in an era when even less was understood than it is now could have held me back. I think educational settings might have underestimated me or assumed that I couldn't do things I could. That's because, from what I discovered, my assessment results were quite unusual and extreme.

It took me a while to get to grips with my hefty report and one thing I learned through reading it was that autistic people often have what is called a 'spiky profile'. This means that we can have things we're really skilled at and also things we struggle with. So, when the results of assessments are plotted on a piece of paper, a neurotypical person will have a relatively straight horizontal line with perhaps the odd bump, peak or trough here and there. Conversely, I and others like me are likely to have results that go up and down on the page and look like lots of spikes, giving the appearance of a mountain range when the points are joined up. These peaks indicate things that we're particularly good at, and the dips are a testament to the things we're less skilled at or struggle with.

Following my assessment, I discovered that such things as my numeracy left me statistically in the bottom echelons of the population. Conversely, my abilities with language and vocabulary placed me at the top end. Seemingly, to have such a huge disparity in a set of results was very unusual.

I am either very good at something or very poor. By way of an example, I struggle with sequencing. For some people, sequencing could relate to alphabetical order, directions, how numbers relate to one another, or perhaps patterns in numbers. Which disability this relates to in me, I don't know because when you have a smörgåsbord, or 'buffet of disabilities' to choose from, it's difficult to know where one condition starts and another ends. This is also complicated because there are commonalities across conditions such as dyslexia and dyscalculia.

Nonetheless, it was particularly problematic for me in the workplace trying to explain to somebody that while I could write legally complicated and detailed representations for a client, or explain an intricate legal matter to somebody with cognitive difficulties, I couldn't accurately put a court bundle of documents and papers together because of the problems I had with working out what went where, despite it being a straightforward task for many. I faced much criticism because some people thought I didn't want to do it because I saw it as too menial. This certainly wasn't the case. I found it incredibly difficult.

I suspect either being really good at something or really poor assisted the masking of my conditions and masked my difficulties to those around me. I shall explain more about masking shortly.

I think the starkness of the extremes of my report is also evident in my personality. If I were a food, I'd be a Scotch bonnet chilli, and if I were to be a haircut, I'd be a Mohican.

I feel that I have always been the exception to the rule. If a clinical trial consisting of one million people were to show that a medication worked in 99% of all cases, I would be in the 1% group.

I'm the 'i' before 'e' except after 'c' when that rule doesn't apply, like with such words as 'weird', 'feisty' and 'foreign'. When people say, "What usually happens" or "It should be fine", you can guarantee it doesn't apply to me. I am the person who needs two courses of antibiotics because the ones given to the vast majority of people cannot get to grips with me. I was also born in the era of confectionery laden with sugar, additives and E numbers, and yet have no fillings in my teeth. In fact, I still have two baby teeth in situ!

Like most people in school, I'd gravitated towards subjects I was good at, such as humanities, but now, during my legal training, when I couldn't pick and choose to play to my strengths, basic balance sheets, accounts and simple formulae for tax calculations were anathemas to me. I'd always loved learning about history and literature, and what bit I didn't immediately grasp didn't matter, because I had something else – a visual memory.

Pictorially, I could recall information and images and almost 'replay' them in my mind like a video. So, the discussion held in class around a concept or recalling the explanation given by a tutor to a student enabled me to 'revisit' things I hadn't been able to grasp or process at the time.

I'd developed coping strategies without even knowing it. I'd remember where my fellow class members were positioned in which room and could even recall what clothing they wore at the time. I'd say my memory had compensated for many of my shortcomings in the classroom.

From a young age, I'd mastered memorising voluminous quantities of data. That information could be facts, routes, conversations, methods or exactly where my favourite chocolate bars were on the sweetshop shelf. My recall was seldom based on knowledge or understanding; it was based on pure visual memory. As a small child, I struggled as I had yet to hone this skill and make it work for me. I'd always possessed the ability, but mastering it as I got older would be essential if I was to keep up and get on.

As I aged, I passed exams through my ability to arrange everything I knew into a series of images on the revision page. That way, I could 'read off' from my mental picture gallery and 'pull out' whatever information I needed for the respective question and 'plug' it into my answer. I did this in the first instance by designing the page containing the revision information to be 'visually recall-friendly'. That way, I could ensure that it was accessible on command in an exam.

So, in some respects, I'd unknowingly devised coping strategies, but I'd also camouflaged a problem. That said, I've always preferred to see opportunities before problems, so I'll say that I 'upcycled' the skill and made it work for me.

As a preschool child, I could find a house I'd been to with my mum just once before. Even if she couldn't recall its location, I could. I remembered where the rows of shops were, the letter box locations, bus shelter positions and even the road signs, which I couldn't yet read. I didn't just remember them; I remembered them in respect of their proximity to something else memorable. Each object was a reference point to the next and I felt rewarded each time I was correct about the next reference point. I'd think in pictures and do so to this day.

I can recall my auntie's flat I entered at age two in graphic detail. I can still remember the exact floor plan and where furniture and ornaments were located. The 1970s and 1980s saw a lot of multicoloured soft furnishings and carpets, and I remember the colour and texture of these, too. I would take the time to look at the individual swirls of different shades, tones and colours within the carpet pile and note how each fitted into the larger pattern. I can remember the red leather-topped drum stool in the kitchen corner and how I marvelled at its cylindrical shape. I can remember the heavily raised patterned sofa upholstery and the exact location of the cigarette burns. I didn't know that they were fag burns, but I did wonder why there were dry, frilly circles at random intervals on the sofa, which didn't appear to have a function or purpose.

I liked the orange with green ceramic tiles making up the surface of the coffee table and the half-full red glass Murano ashtray occupying the centre. As I recall the images, the smells return, too.

Curry powder.

Ammonia aromas began exactly two steps from the toilet door.

Cigarette smoke, old and new.

Remembering minutiae was only the beginning. I could and still do take enormous pleasure from things, particularly very small things, things which others may overlook. I can be mesmerised by a very particular shade of colour, gripped by a single component of a smell or a taste of a wine or perfume and transfixed by a tiny section of a piece of music. In fact, when I first fall in love with a fragment of music, I can play that few seconds maybe fifty-plus times, until I know every element and nuance.

We're still at the edge of understanding autism and its countless manifestations. What's more, while some books and films have done much to raise the profile of autism on the whole, there are some people who assume we're all savants. The vast majority of us are not and spend a lot of time saying, "How the hell am I supposed to know what day of the week it was on this day in 1863?", or impolitely declining duplicitous offers to go to a casino and play Blackjack.

I don't want the understanding of autism to be just limited to those with a special interest in those of us with a 'special interest'. I'd like to enable a few more people to understand more about autism's all-too-esoteric complexities.

Furthermore, everybody's neurodivergence (be that autism, ADHD, dyslexia, dyspraxia, dyscalculia, etc.) is the same *until* it's different, and it's always different.

That said, you don't need to understand everything about everybody's particular condition(s). You just need to work out what you need to know to work, live, get along with, help and support that individual, because every person *is* an individual. Don't just see the conditions because there's a person there, too.

Neurodivergent people need to fathom out their own coping strategies to get through the day, but this can take time. However, I think the same applies to the neurotypical person insofar as *they* need to develop almost secondary coping strategies because they need to understand how best to understand and, where necessary, help the neurodivergent person. So, I think we have to 'help the helpers' and equip them with a clear window of insight because, for too long, the glass has been opaque, and while some have been doing their best to clear the fog and drive away the mist, the ignorance of others has hindered us for long enough.

Increasing numbers of people are receiving diagnoses, and even more are in the wings. If I can improve understanding, challenge a few misconceptions and lay a bit of paving on an otherwise hazardous potholed path, then I shall be quietly pleased with myself.

Adjustments: Who's making them for whom?

Regardless of the law, we help people with disabilities. We hope as human beings that society will make 'adjustments' for us because it's the right thing to do. However, I've always thought that it was the other way around and that *we,* those of us who are neurodivergent, actually have to adjust for neurotypicals. This is because *they* are the mainstream, and we live in *their* world, which is governed by *their* terms of reference and what *they* think is 'normal'.

Neurotypicals dictate and determine societal norms and how we should and should not behave or live our lives. They dictate what is expected and what is and is not acceptable. So, if I want to live in their multicoloured world with my black-and-white thinking, and fit in, and get through life, I need to change and become more 'normal', more like them.

So, who is making the adjustments for whom?

Many people will (and I think autistic girls are better than autistic boys in my experience) 'mirror' the behaviours of others who they think appear to know how it all works, which will enable them to integrate. Therefore, by 'masking' the more obvious features of their neurodivergence, they can spend less time with their head below the parapet, fit in and appear less odd. But masking comes at a price and is not without consequences.

Masking is when we feel the need, consciously or unconsciously, to go to considerable lengths to camouflage and suppress aspects of our personality and the manifestations of our neurodivergence. If you have met an autistic person in a social setting, they may well have been masking, presenting a veneer of what they felt was the most appropriate way to behave in the current circumstances.

They could seek to mask these facets which could be stimming, (a repetitive movement used for self-regulation or self-soothing), talking about a special interest or avoiding social interactions. Examples of stimming can include hand and finger movements, rocking or jumping around. Stimming can also be less obvious, such as hair twirling or foot tapping. A special interest may change or may never change. It may be joined by other special interests, too. A special interest isn't just a hobby or having a favourite television programme you love. It's a highly focused interest which not only brings great joy to the autistic person, but can also help manage and regulate their anxiety. In a child, a special interest could be a subject such as the solar system, dinosaurs or an object like a toy car. It's no different for adults, although the examples may change. The vast majority of autistic people will have a special interest. That said, what this is and how it changes and develops is as unique as the individual themself.

In my case, one of the things I try to mask is my poor eye contact. For so many neurotypicals, eye contact is the most natural thing to do. It's expected and seen as a sign of sincerity, but for me, it's excruciating. It feels like I'm having a laser pen shone in my eyes when I meet another set of human eyes. Strangely enough, though, I find animal eyes just fine.

We go to massive lengths to emulate the 'normals' in the hope that we can fit into their world and function in their atmosphere.

So, if we can minimise those features that make us stand out and frustrate our ability to comply with society's expectations, our lives may be a little easier. We may then be considered as a candidate for a job or an interesting task at work, or the person we're attracted to may go on a date with us, or if we're in school, we might not get picked on as much.

However, not everyone masters these coping strategies or even wants to. Some are tired of adhering to a set of unspoken rules they may not understand. Some feel they are inconsistent with their values, and some of us find them draining. Sometimes the mask slips too, because it's so difficult to consistently maintain a façade, which is exactly what it is for most of us. Imagine somebody from the twenty-first century spending the rest of their life playing the role of Shakespeare's Iago, or Othello or Hamlet – every day. But that's what it can be like for us. We need to put on a 'social costume' and play a character who will fit in and not get ridiculed or picked on.

What's more, as authenticity is so central to us and integral in our decision-making, we can feel like we're being disingenuous by masking and that creates a real dilemma. We rely so much on the honesty and integrity of others because we naturally take things literally or at face value. Therefore, things need to be what they seem, because if they're not, we're liable to become seriously discombobulated.

Coping strategies

When navigating my way through the neurotypical world, I not only have to make adjustments for the 'normals', but I have had to develop various means of managing my own difficulties. This is to circumvent the all too numerous perils and pitfalls to avoid additional stress, because a neurodivergent life is a stressful and hazardous one.

I spend my days avoiding bright lights, loud or high-pitched noises, scratchy fabrics, clicking pens, being hot, socialising, small talk, hypocrisy and disingenuous people. I like vertical lists, order, clarity, detail, routine, punctuality, symmetry, honesty and limited contact with people, especially their eyes.

Life is full of all the things I try to avoid and the things I need are too frequently in short supply, so like many autistic people, I have developed coping strategies. These aren't a magic pill nor do they mitigate the things which are most problematic to me; however, they do help to make my life a little bit easier in terms of crippling anxiety management and accomplishing tasks.

These coping strategies change as one travels on life's voyage. I can do things now that I couldn't previously grasp and while practice doesn't make perfect, it's made things good enough in my case.

By way of an example, I struggle enormously with my numeracy. I may deploy different means to achieve an end goal compared to the 'normals' and I may not like undertaking the task, but I do like repetition and the pursuit of perfection. This at times extreme repetition of practice not only helps me manage my stress levels but also usually gets me where I need to be in terms of passing an exam or completing a task.

I particularly struggled with the accounting component of my legal training in the classroom, to the extent that I'd go through the examples handed out in class seventy-plus times at home, whereas my fellow classmates had it mastered in a couple of practice runs. Nonetheless, I passed and looking at my results on paper, you wouldn't think that I was any different from the other students, but if you knew what it had taken to get there, it was quite staggering.

While some people have been brilliant and have helped me more than I could ever have asked for, sadly I've had to deal with varying degrees of sneering, usually from people who should know better. That said, I always get there in the end, and the disappointing responses of others have unfortunately been a reflection of their shortcomings and not mine.

For me, there are countless 'stress generators'. These are things which are very stressful for me but would probably not stress a neurotypical, for example, sameness and consistency. The 'normals' can cope quite well with a change to their routine and are often baffled by the upset this can cause me. I've been told, "That's life!", "Get over it!" and "What's the big deal?" Neurotypicals don't tend to be disrupted by change, but we do. They don't require those around them to understand the need for things to be a certain way and the stress it causes if this isn't understood or is minimised.

This lack of appreciation stems from the fact that things which are paramount to us aren't paramount to them. Some things may be annoying or get on a 'normal's' nerves, but I've never seen a neurotypical adversely impacted by having their daily routine disrupted, or by not being able to sit at the same desk, or having to sit by somebody loudly eating crunchy, strong-smelling food.

Avoiding or at least managing these stress generators is imperative for us, and the ability to do so plays an enormous part in the life of somebody who just sometimes needs to get through the day. Having developed some kind of 'toolkit', we ask that these tools aren't blunted or buckled unnecessarily.

Some of my best friends are autistic

Really?

As you might appreciate, this is about as comforting to an autistic person as it is to a black person, when people feel the need to demonstrate that they're definitely, *definitely* not at all racist.

One of the most difficult groups of neurotypicals to deal with is those who *think* they understand autism, but really don't. They are similar to heterosexual people who attend Pride and say, "Yes, I understand homophobia. I love the gays – they're hilarious. We had a great time in San Francisco and we're off to Mykonos next year."

They may find homophobia abhorrent. However, I fail to see how they could ever begin to appreciate the lived and often daily experience of casual homophobia. Similarly, I wouldn't dream of watching a documentary on Nelson Mandela and then going on to assume I understand racism and what it's like to grow up subjected to apartheid.

Another group who get on my nerves are those who make a token attempt to understand, perhaps because they have to. They greet you with tea and sympathy and think they can consider themselves sensitive to you and the needs of your type. They believe they're fully compliant, an ally, and could never be criticised for being discriminatory because they've been on the internet and read a bit about autism, have a direct debit in favour of neglected donkeys, go to church, and no longer use words such as 'spastic'.

I've witnessed racism from people who wouldn't dream of using the N-word to describe a black person. I've seen sexism from people who'd frown at a vulgar mother-in-law joke and misogyny from politically correct devotees. Let's be clear; a lot of discrimination goes on between those who genuinely understand and embrace equality while making adjustments, and those who describe all Indians using the P word. It's a big void in which to get a lot wrong.

Outside of the circle

I have always been an outsider looking in. If you're an outsider, you're different and notice different things, things other people take for granted or don't see. I would not say that I am an observer, but I am a noticer, especially of small things. Small things appear small, but when you look at them and into them, they are quite often massive.

These small things can be inanimate objects, situations, events or even people. I then like to watch how these small things influence other things and ultimately have a domino effect. For me, the detail of the minutiae is fascinating because it's so revealing and usually huge.

I've been considered 'diplomatically incontinent' by some of those 'inside of the circle'. This is because I'm brutally honest and frank with my opinions and have no problem answering a question without attaching any kind of glossy veneer. I call it authenticity, and they call it rude.

I think this is because I have my own particular brand of disdain for diplomacy at the expense of honesty and integrity. In the first instance, it goes against my values but also leaves me utterly confused and wading through infinite possibilities. I think being diplomatic is a form of masking, and not only does it not say what it means, but it's also shrouded with a variety of potential meanings and intentions. Being discourteous has never been my intention, but when you're honest, hurting somebody's feelings can result in collateral damage.

Sometimes, I am considered rude because I am direct and, to quote certain wounded recipients of my honesty, 'blunt'. So, if you don't want to know if your bum looks big in something, then don't ask me if you don't want an honest answer. If your clothes feel a little bit snugger than they used to, but you want someone to say, "No, you haven't gained an ounce," ask someone willing to polish the reality. Despite frequently offending people, it's never my aim.

Another problem with offending people is that they say they're 'fine' when they're clearly not. I've been told by people I've upset that they're 'fine' through snot bubbles and borderline hyperventilation. They're clearly not 'fine', so why they do this, I don't know, because it's dishonest.

I once remember a colleague complaining how she needed to get her roots sorted and having had my attention drawn to them, I confirmed that she was correct and that they did indeed need addressing if she wanted to conceal her grey. Evidently, it was a statement on her behalf, not an invitation to comment.

While we were on the subject, I also enquired as to whether she had intentionally chosen to have her hair that particular shade of ginger to match her beloved spaniel or whether it was just a coincidence. After the gulps, gasps and sharp intakes of breath had subsided around the room, she too was 'fine' about my enquiry and confirmed that she didn't dye or cut her hair to match her dog's fur. However, you'd never have known that she was 'fine', as her face was as red as her and her spaniel's locks for the rest of the afternoon.

Once I've been fallen out with, I'm never sure how long it'll be until things return to normal, which is frustrating for somebody who likes to know what's happening and when. In the past, when I've caused upset and been fallen out with, I have tried to ask for some kind of timetable as to when things will return to how they were, because I don't like my routine being disrupted. However, upset people seem reluctant to say how many hours/days/weeks it'll take for normality to resume, which is unfortunate. I'm sure I've been cancelled countless times; however, I remain none the wiser.

There have been various attempts at rebranding my thinking and approach to matters, all of which failed miserably because being disarmingly frank and honest is just how I am.

In recent years, when people have set up 'group chats' on messaging platforms, I've found myself being added in without my consent. I find these groups similar to a digital social event and have no desire whatsoever to be there. Occasionally, I have returned to my phone after being away for no more than an hour to find over one hundred messages, all about clothes, boyfriends or reality programmes on television I know nothing about.

I wouldn't mind so much being added to a group that discussed historical documentaries or politics, but having to read about people 'lol' and post emojis depicting faces, which invariably mean nothing to me, is like adding a high-profile female influencer into a group chat dedicated to discussing cement mixers or combine harvesters which she's unlikely to be interested in.

I tolerated being in these groups for a while, but they took over my phone, so I left. Now, I leave immediately as soon as I'm added in as a participant, which has raised a few eyebrows, literally. However, I can't continue to pretend I'm interested in the content and would rather be considered antisocial.

I've never felt the need to fill in the so-called 'awkward gaps' or 'prolonged silences' in conversations. I'm quite happy to let them remain, expand or morph into a large vortex of quietness. I've seen people agree to all sorts of things or say something incongruous just to avoid what they consider to be an excruciating level of invisible discomfort, which neurotypicals tend to feel, usually, I'm told, located in the core.

I have often wanted to stop them, but a 'normal's' need to regain inner composure is greater than the inconvenience of having agreed to take on something they really didn't want to do. Next time you're in one of these situations, just try and refrain from offering to drive fifty miles out of your way or taking on an extra mountain of work just so you don't feel like you're dying on the inside and having to go through sixteen shades of awkward. It may cause discomfort in the first instance, but I think some of you 'normals' could get better at it with practice and become less of a dumping ground.

Take my word for it: I've spent years 'rehearsing' what I have to do to comply with neurotypicals, and it'd be good if they could learn something from us. I think it could also work well with other things, like saying no to a further date. Don't make up a big story or elaborate circumstances about minding your friend's neighbour's dog; say no. Nicely, but no.

Honesty and integrity

From a young age, we're taught that honesty, integrity, trustworthiness and transparency are qualities we should adhere to and live by. A sense of 'fair play' and 'doing the right thing' are virtues bestowed upon many from early on in life and even if they don't come naturally, they're certainly aspirational and encouraged.

However, it appears that only some of this is true, sometimes and in certain situations. It's not written down anywhere, and nobody really can agree upon when it should be adhered to in full, or when a flexible approach can be adopted, the latter being called 'white lies'.

I have a huge problem with honesty and integrity in the sense that the 'normals' possess a somewhat malleable approach to these 'core values', which tend to be referred to as such, but only when it suits. If the world were more honest, life would be so much easier for the neurodivergent, because we often take things at face value, which can be especially hazardous, particularly in the work environment.

I used to work for a local authority in legal services and was once tasked with selling charity raffle tickets at Christmas. As I went around the building, I asked the names of everyone who bought one, along with their department and role, so they could be easily located if they won. As I'd done on previous occasions, I asked one lady for her details. When it came to her role, she said she worked in "Ethics and Values", to which I said, "That's great. When are we getting some?"

I think that she thought it was my attempt at a joke. However, my question was genuine based on some of the behaviours and conduct of certain staff I'd witnessed since I'd worked there. If I'd have turned as many blind eyes as some people did to the misdemeanours of others around them, I'd have a Labrador guide dog and white stick by now.

Although many claim that honesty and integrity are at their core, when it's pointed out with examples that they or those whose behaviour they're turning a blind eye to aren't living to the very values they espouse, they don't like it. But why? I thought honesty was paramount.

We're all a bit autistic, aren't we?

In a word, no.

When people have discovered that I'm neurodivergent, I've had everything from, "Oh bless!" to "It's a shame." I don't need a blessing, and the only shame is that others behave as they do. Then I've had people say, "I wouldn't worry about having a bit of autism." The next thing people do is tell me, "We're all a bit autistic, you know?" which, of course, we're not and is like saying, "We're all a little bit pregnant."

One of the favourite pastimes of the 'normals' when they meet an autistic person is to try and ascertain where you are on the mysterious 'spectrum' that 'we're all on', and each person places you somewhere different. Sometimes, it feels like being a donkey upon which a load of uninformed, well-meaning, blindfolded people are trying to pin a tail. Everybody puts the tail in a different place, too, and for the most part, it's nowhere near the donkey's rear.

Ableism

Ableism is more than discrimination to me. It advances the idea that somebody who is disabled is somehow inferior when compared to somebody without a disability and what's more, they really could do with being fixed or sorted out.

It's the view that there is a 'right' and a 'wrong' way for people to be, usually based upon 'the norm', a category they fit into. Anybody who deviates from their perceived idea of what is correct is deemed somehow inferior in their mind. This is made especially difficult because, in my experience, it's seldom intentional. It's undoubtedly lazy and uninformed, but most people are decent and don't get up on a morning to offend or discriminate, and if they knew they had, they'd be horrified.

Sometimes, it can be oh so subtle and therefore very difficult to evidence because it could be a tone, a roll of the eyes, language or even just a pursed lip. Of course, on other occasions, it can be as subtle as a blunt force trauma, but for the most part, from what I've seen concerning myself and others, it's executed by those who have no idea that their words or conduct are exclusive, harmful and regressive.

When I was first diagnosed, I was quickly 're-diagnosed' by others with no relevant qualifications whatsoever as 'high functioning'. I think this was partly an attempt to mollify me because they assumed I must need a boost being in receipt of this crushing news.

The premise of the comment was that I wasn't 'low functioning', so I should count my blessings. I soon learned that, in their mind, I wasn't non-verbal or profoundly affected by the condition. After all, it could be worse. I didn't live in residential care, have an emergency panic cord in my home which immediately brought me to the attention of a warden, or have a grown-up provided by adult social care to help me manage my finances or take me shopping in the community. I was married. I was educated. I had a job. I could converse. Okay, I might be a bit odd and idiosyncratic, but so are lots of people.

To set autistic people against one another in this way creates a good versus bad, useful versus burdensome kind of narrative, and it's not just incorrect. It's harmful. Rather than thinking about autism as a point on a vertical line, I think of it as a collection of colours on a painter's palette, all of which come into contact with one another at some point. That way, you can see that it's not X that marks the spot where somebody graduates into 'high functioning' or slips into 'low functioning'; it's more circular with no beginning, middle or end.

By saying somebody is 'high functioning', their daily difficulties and battles can be minimised or dismissed altogether. Conversely, the 'low functioning' person may struggle with verbal communication. However, this doesn't mean they're unintelligent or can't do something you can do. They may even be better.

We process information differently

Sometimes, it can take us longer to process information. I'd say the best way to explain it is like a car journey. If somebody wanted to get from Glasgow to Edinburgh, they'd probably get onto the M8 motorway and follow the road until they reached their destination. It's a straight road which will take you directly there.

However, as an autistic person, I may start on the M8, then get onto a few of the A roads, visit a stately home I've read about that looked interesting, and rejoin the M8. I then might deviate onto some of the B roads for a while. I'll still get to Edinburgh, but it can take me a bit longer because I've needed to utilise some of the minor roads off the main highway. This doesn't mean I'm not listening, and this isn't a choice I have; it's just a different way of reaching Edinburgh. The reason it takes a bit longer isn't because I'm 'slow' or 'stupid'. It's because I consider other bits of information en route. It's not optional; it's how we're wired.

Receiving, processing and understanding information can be problematic for me, too and by that, I mean all sorts of information. This could be from when somebody is angry with me but not saying so, to social cues, to verbal instructions, to when I am not supposed to say something that everybody else has somehow 'picked up on', presumably through the process of osmosis.

Neurotypicals convey information through so many different methods. They may say nothing at all; they may place their face in unnatural positions, gesticulate, deploy hand signals and generate noises, all of which clearly mean something to those around them, but often not to those of us who are autistic.

Deciphering and untangling body language are very difficult, especially as neurotypicals seem to have an inbuilt Enigma cipher machine, much like the one Alan Turing cracked during WWII, which seems to decode everything for them so easily and quickly.

There's such a huge labyrinth of unspoken information conveyed by neurotypicals and it can be utterly bewildering because we can often be left mystified and perplexed, while searching for something more tangible and familiar to latch onto.

Meanwhile, the poor neurotypical sod, who has so intuitively delivered the information in the best way they instinctively know how, can't understand why they're not being understood because they think they've been really clear; they think that smirk or shrug did the trick, but it didn't, and they're not sure why.

I've been called "obtuse", "difficult" and "stupid" because, to others, it's just plain obvious, but it isn't to us; it's another language, and there's no online translation software for a raised eyebrow or frown.

Faces are and remain a conundrum to me. I only wish there were some formula to quickly work them out. What is elementary and taken for granted by my neurotypical counterparts continues to flummox me. From what I'm led to believe, I'm supposed to be able to tell how someone is feeling, what they're thinking, their mood or even whether they like something or not.

Faces tell me little of that.

A face is the front part of the head, the bit that looks outwards and while some are more appealing than others, the way they are moved and contorted reveals little, if anything to me about the thoughts and feelings of the occupant. For me, they are functional and hold some of the senses and not much more.

Neurodivergent people often have different learning styles because we absorb information differently. Although we may appear inflexible or resistant to change, we crave familiarity, so if we've discovered or devised a formula enabling us to complete a task, cope with a situation or learn something new, let us get on with it. Don't try and get us to do it like everyone else does it, because that is similar to when left-handed people were forced to write with their right hand, and what did that achieve?

Monotropism: The toilet roll telescope

Monotropism means a constrained range of interests and is a characteristic feature of autism.

I describe it to people, relaying my childhood love of the used toilet roll cardboard tube I redeployed as a makeshift telescope. You can only see what's at the end of the empty tube, and there's no peripheral vision, so you're drawn only to what you can locate at the end. You can't see anything else unless you shift the tube.

So, if you can get your head around the 'telescope' concept, you'll understand so much more about why autistic people think as we do.

Monotropism, like many things connected with autism, has pros and cons. I've concluded that there are some real advantages to it because of its connection to why we're good at focusing on one thing and doing it really well. However, because we live in a world that isn't configured to operate like us or understand how and why we go about things differently, its features can be viewed through a negative prism.

From what I have read about monotropism, I'd say that it facilitates my ability to hyperfocus on a task, so much so that I can become engrossed in it, regardless of people, space or time. I look at it from every angle and almost want to 'reverse engineer' it.

However, the consequence of this is that it can exclude everything and anything else. I focus on one thing at a time because I only have the capacity for singular thinking, so multi-focusing or multitasking isn't an option. If I'm forced to be 'cognitively flexible', it won't work, and I'm liable to become confused and stressed.

As human beings, we absorb information from lots of different places, from different senses and in different ways. Conversely, neurotypicals are sometimes described as polytropic because they can absorb lots of different information from different sources and don't have the 'toilet roll telescope' to contend with.

So, for example, they could be watching television with someone, periodically conversing and responding to a text, all while having something to eat. Or, they could be listening to music, notice something out of the window and then somebody speaks, during which time they continue to make a sandwich.

A great deal going on there requires an individual to assimilate many different types of information in different ways simultaneously. Many neurotypicals won't give it a second thought and will have taken everything on board. I'm more of a 'one thing at a time' kind of person, and many autistic people are.

The downside of this is that sometimes, especially when we're receiving instructions or learning something new, we may need multiple stimuli or bits of information from different places to understand something, and that's especially challenging for us.

This is then made all the more problematic if the instructor, teacher, trainer or employer, for example, doesn't know or doesn't take the time (say in my case) to allow me to make notes, or they speak quickly or in imprecise terms, or they become frustrated if I seek to clarify something. Or, worst of all, they'll tell me I'm not listening. Hands up if you'd tell someone with scoliosis to stop slouching and stand up straight. Or perhaps you'd suggest that the fibromyalgia sufferer stops making a fuss and should just go and take a paracetamol tablet?

Neurotypicals are like a car because a car is a machine designed to undertake many different functions simultaneously. A car can maintain a constant speed of seventy mph while the indicators, lights, radio, cruise control, electric windows and A/C all operate concurrently and in perfect harmony. Neurotypicals are very similar in that they can bring skills together to achieve an aim. I can do all of those things, but not necessarily simultaneously, and any attempt to enforce it will result in my feeling overwhelmed, overloaded and wiped out.

I've seen neurodivergent people 'mask' to conceal their embarrassment at not taking it all in at once. Just by a neurotypical taking some extra time to ensure they've explained things clearly, they can make a real difference. Not taking the time with someone who needs it and expecting them to 'run with' a set of garbled instructions is akin to my asking a neurotypical to juggle seven balls, hop on one leg, scratch their ear, stir a cup of tea and sing a song backwards, all at the same time.

Now that I understand monotropism a bit more, I think or possibly feel it is like a sieve. When you pour water into the sieve and are neurotypical, the water flows through very easily. There are many holes; the water isn't competing for an outlet and quickly and easily finds an exit point.

Conversely, as an autistic person, I feel that our thinking is more like trying to pour a can of chunky vegetable soup through the sieve. Some of the liquid will come through, but there'll be an awful lot of diced carrots, potatoes and peas left at the bottom, which won't be going anywhere. Those vegetables left in the sieve are all the stuff we didn't pick up on. So, we need help to ensure there's as little as possible left behind.

Reductive of difference

I think many adults can downplay the manifestations of their neurodivergence because they don't want to stand out any more than necessary, especially for the 'wrong' reasons.

Think about when you've met an extremely tall person or somebody with a strange voice; you remember them for that one reason as opposed to perhaps the more important fact that they cured your chest infection, fixed your boiler or did a brilliant job of cutting your hair. We don't always want our autism to define us because other things about us could be more important or interesting.

I have been guilty of minimising features of my neurodivergence when met with scepticism or downright prejudice, because I know that people may think I'm unable to carry out a task or it'll take too long to explain it to me so it's just easier for that opportunity to be afforded to somebody else.

Many workplaces aren't adequately set up for the neurodivergent, and what's more, if we want the chance, for example, to be involved in something interesting, please equip us with what we need to give it our best shot and become involved, rather than taking the course of least resistance because you think it's simpler. You might surprise yourself because we might surprise you, and I think that the neurotypical world has lost out on what we have to offer for too long.

Remember, only 29% of autistic adults are employed, and this needs to change.

Synaesthesia: Come to your senses

Synaesthesia is a neurological condition thought to be genetic, so it's likely to be passed on from parent to child. The word synaesthesia originates from the Greek meaning 'to perceive together'. Information meant to stimulate one sense stimulates another, so senses which aren't normally connected become so.

For example, you could taste a colour or letters, and numbers could be a colour for you. One person may envisage the letter 'G' as pink, or the colour blue may have a particular taste. The day Wednesday could be orange. You may be able to smell a shape or feel a sound.

Scientists believe the condition occurs in a significantly larger proportion of autistic people compared to neurotypical people. Providing accurate statistics is difficult because so many autistic people remain undiagnosed. Even if a child were to have synaesthesia, they may not realise that what they are experiencing is unusual.

Synaesthesia certainly isn't exclusive to autism, but it is more prevalent in those with autism, and so that's why it's the basis for the title of this book.

Sensory overload

This can feel like drowning, and it's challenging to manage, so I do my utmost to avoid it, but it's not always possible. I can experience a sensory overload when my senses are simultaneously subjected to too much information, although sometimes straightforward 'people overload' can rapidly overwhelm me.

I would most liken it to an intense multiple sensory assault or violation. I may not behave like a child does when they have 'overload'. Nonetheless, I can really struggle to manage it and although I can become very restless and fidgety, my meltdowns are largely internalised. They're more like shutdowns.

A sensory overload can come about in a variety of situations. For example, when multiple conversations occur simultaneously, or even worse, when two different music pieces are played simultaneously. When this happens, I feel like my skin is being turned inside out, slowly from the inside.

I can only wear certain fabric types as I'm very sensitive to how it feels, so it must be soft. Otherwise, it's physically untenable. I also have to remove all the labels from my clothes and place them in a bowl along with a note attached to them, stating what items of clothing they belong to.

Colours can also overwhelm me, and I can feel them deeply. I think the brightest, most overwhelming colour in the world is yellow, and although beautiful, I have to treat it with caution; less is more. It's a bit like seasoning food with salt and pepper. A small amount enhances the food, but that little bit too much ruins it and makes it unpalatable and I have to push the plate away.

Then there's the sleep battle, and that's the mother of all wars because it invariably compounds sensory overload and leaves me more likely to need to withdraw from people or 'shut down'. Poor sleep is the one feature I probably struggle with the most because not only is it difficult at the time but it's awful the next day, and the problem is only exacerbated and compounded over time, as my desperate need for sleep, and craving to switch off, mushrooms.

I'm a diabolical sleeper and always have been. Nothing works; even total exhaustion is often insufficient to knock me out. I try very hard but the ability to just drop off or wake up feeling refreshed has always eluded me. I suspect that I have a sleep debt, which, if converted into economic terms, would leave me with the debt-to-GDP ratio of Venezuela.

You'd think after a day of masking and trying not to say the wrong thing, coupled with heightened anxiety and residual burnout, I'd drift off into a peaceful slumber. No. It doesn't work like that. That's when the ADHD makes an entrance, kicks off, demands attention and starts making plans, reviews the day, reminds me of things I need to do and leaves my brain feeling like a racetrack, except the cars don't all necessarily travel in the same direction.

We're hidden in plain sight

I think one of the greatest battles faced by those of us who are neurodivergent is that such things as autism or dyslexia are largely invisible. You can't see, hear or touch them. Of course, there can be giveaway characteristics such as hand flapping, poor eye contact or pedantic speech, but as a general rule, it can be difficult to tell somebody who is autistic from somebody who is not, especially in the first instance.

In my opinion, this is both a blessing and a hindrance. This is a blessing because, in passing, the condition isn't likely to be obvious and liable to attract curious glances from onlookers, as can happen to people with physical disabilities. At the same time, it is a curse. There's a misconception that you're 'normal' or 'okay', and so you should act in an anticipated way and say appropriate things at a suitable time, as per the social norms laid down by the 'normals'.

What's more, I can find people's attitudes towards me so disempowering. Having read an article about autism or seen a TV programme about it, or more commonly, none of the above, I can find people think that they've mastered autism, or worse still, it's just 'bad behaviour' or I am 'just being awkward'.

I am still incensed when people say things like, "It'll do you good..." or "What's best for you, is..." when they have little to no appreciation of the manifestations of my conditions and how these affect me and people like me. We are not autism's answer to mendacious malingering. The disability (and in my opinion, it *is* a disability) is genuine and it doesn't always make for comfortable viewing.

Making such ignorant declarations doesn't just minimise, for example, autism and its impact, but can also disempower the autistic person. How can somebody with little to no insight make such claims with any credence? It's like putting a quadriplegic in a wheelchair at the bottom of a flight of stairs and saying, "Go on, have a go; you'll never know unless you try. You might even surprise yourself." Nor would you take the handles of a wheelchair without being asked to and wheel the occupant in your chosen direction. Sometimes, neurotypicals show an alarming lack of insight – and they say we miss the signs.

By the time you come to the end of this book, I hope, if nothing else, that through the laughs and gasps, you will see that a disability doesn't invalidate a person; indeed, I think it can fortify.

Burdened with my smörgåsbord of challenges referenced in this chapter and only a short while after being diagnosed, I embarked upon my new career as a trainee solicitor in an impoverished urban landscape that Westminster had long forgotten. This was where I first met Brenda.

Chapter 2
Brenda

Having spent some time in a few different law firms, I had acquired some impressions of what a solicitor's office was like. I shadowed different lawyers in different areas of legal expertise to see what area I might like to work in. Some of the firms I visited were more affluent than others. Nonetheless, the firms I'd spent a small amount of time in were generally well-organised and appropriate regarding staff and the office environment.

Moreover, I'd previously worked for a multinational organisation for a number of years, so I had a reasonable understanding of what one might expect from the workplace. I understood professionalism and the day-to-day running of a business, from HR and marketing to budgets and profit making. However, this was a place that flew in the face of my previous encounters with the world of work, and much of that was connected with Brenda and her conduct.

I didn't arrive at the office at the beginning, middle or end of any particular period; I just partook in some of the journey. The merry-go-round was just as much in full swing when I jumped on as when I jumped off. In the grand scheme of things, I clambered on, clung on tightly, qualified as a solicitor, jumped off and had my eyes opened and my values reassessed. The experience undoubtedly had a massive impact on me.

Before working there, I had never been privy to such a world. I hadn't known poverty nor belonged to a family with an array of criminal antecedents or had local authority involvement in my upbringing. The closest I ever got to prison was when we drove past the local borstal as a child, and I was threatened with a prolonged stay if my behaviour didn't improve.

Of course, I knew such places existed, but only in the same way as I know that there's a whole solar system out there that I've never visited. I'd never been anywhere like this before, just as I've never been outside the earth's atmosphere. I think it's fair to say that my experience of this new world was through the 'wrong' end of a telescope.

Here was somewhere that flouted many of the social norms I'd understood and spent ages trying to master. So, I had to quickly relearn and adjust to a different set of social rules, which were, once again, determined by people unlike me. It was like learning a new language just so I could try and get on. And yet, this was not only a new language; it was an obscure dialect full of irregular verbs, silent letters that aren't pronounced, and an array of incomprehensible linguistic anomalies.

Like a foreigner, I had a palpable 'accent' and it was obvious to many that I wasn't native, but at least I could understand and be understood. Spending each day making adjustments for neurotypicals is exhausting, and it felt disingenuous because it was like adopting a veneer and not being authentic.

When I arrived at the office on a morning, I could only liken it to having to wear a bra which was three sizes too small, along with a thong while suffering from a yeast infection and haemorrhoids. When it was home time, I may have looked more tired and facially distorted than a Picasso painting, but it was like the relentless and unyielding thong had turned into comfy pants, and the bra no longer had a ruthless bone digging into my armpit or vice-like clamp around my circumference.

To understand what daily life was like, firstly, you would have to understand Brenda and the 'Brendafication' of the office.

Officially, Brenda was the manager. However, she was so much more. Brenda's energy and ethos seeped into every crevasse of the organisation. She was pivotal to the firm's culture, and nothing happened at any level without her sanctioning or endorsement. Whether somebody wanted to move a desk or something more substantial, it had to be filtered through Brenda's mindset. If she was feeling buoyant, it wasn't a problem, and she'd probably agree, with sprinkles and glitter. But no matter how reasonable or minor your request was, it'd be drop-kicked from view if she was annoyed, which was her default position.

Despite not being legally trained, she ran a vertical, top-down operation and as governor, she was at the top, and she'd have no problem reiterating where everyone else sat in the food chain. When I was younger and read about dictatorships, I often wondered why there weren't more rebellions and uprisings. Why didn't people say something and depose the autocrats? Having seen it operating in a microcosm, I now understand why people get on with it.

Brenda presented as an avuncular character with a mellifluous voice, a pink candyfloss hairdo, a hearing aid, and eyes greatly magnified by her very thick glasses, and she was blighted by a ubiquitous, dank cough worthy of a heavy smoker. Upon first meeting, it'd be difficult to envisage that this diminutive, cuddly lady wearing orthopaedic clogs could be anything but delightful. I'd even go as far as to suggest that, on a good day, she could be somewhat charismatic. However, I can also honestly say that I'd rather get my head stuck in railings or repeatedly stub my toe for an entire weekend than it be my turn to be on the wrong side of her. This was because when it *was* your turn, extracting the experience from one's mental glue took some considerable time and it was difficult to get one's emotional fabric to lay flat and uncrumpled once more.

Even when talking in her regular, remarkably soft voice, you'd know she was on the cusp of a meltdown when the angry vein located in her forehead started pounding, as it was a reliable barometer of her mood. You knew if the neck vein went as well, it was all downhill from that point forward, and it was imprudent to roll the dice and engage in conversation, because whatever you said would be wrong. Anyone else who became so angry, so quickly, would be liable to encounter a significant cardiac event, such was the strain on her face, but not Brenda. She went from normal to purple in five seconds flat.

Just as when a volcano is about to erupt, everyone within the locality knew it was about to get messy and would flee like the residents of

Pompeii in 79AD. Most people in the office with whom she had spoken at a pre-explosive time usually presented like they were in a hostage video where all that was missing was a copy of that day's newspaper. By the end of a conversation, you'd be grateful that you'd been allowed to live another day.

Most days, you'd have to think very carefully before you asked her a question or needed to see her. If you were shrewd, you'd have worked out what kind of weekend she'd had, if she was in pain with one of her many ailments and conditions, or if she'd had any kind of bad or even vaguely disappointing news. If the answer was yes to any of the above, you'd be thankful for the client you were due to meet or the prison visit you needed to undertake.

Brenda started at the bottom as an administrator, and if she had remained an administrator, that would probably have been for the best. However, she had morphed. As the firm and areas of practice grew, she took on more roles and responsibilities without many of the requisite skills, and the stronger her grip, the more entrenched she became in every cog of every wheel. Brenda was at the very core of the office and integral to the fabric of the place. This was not only because every aspect of the firm was steeped in her energy, but because it bore her values, practices and beliefs like a giant hallmark. When you entered the building, it was like you were entering her home and you adhered to her house rules.

Very occasionally, people would challenge her, and it was terrifying for observers because although uprisings seldom occurred, everybody knew how it would conclude. I'd liken it to the scene from Tiananmen Square in 1989 when the man stood in front of the tank, and everybody stared in awe and feared for his immediate and long-term safety. Everyone knew it was brave, audacious and undertaken with tremendous courage. But at the same time, it was high risk and reckless and was recalled by future members of staff who weren't even there at the time, but because it became instilled in the firm's folklore, it was well known.

None of the 'tank people' ever lasted long as they were swiftly managed out, probably one of the few things she did with precision. Rumours would be spread about them, while expenses and holiday requests would be 'lost'. I remember witnessing the HR details of a 'tank person' being haemorrhaged, as Brenda trundled around the office dispensing their sensitive and personal information as though it was confetti at a wedding. The 'tank people' didn't hang around. However, to be fair, being a 'tank person' wasn't a prerequisite for having your personal information scattergunned around the place; it was just a risk factor.

Brenda held a stash of 'Sorry You're Leaving' cards in her cabinet; such was the regularity with which she required one. Sometimes, she'd buy one with somebody specific in mind, with the individual having no idea at that point that they were going anywhere at all. One day, I took her a cup of tea, and she proudly showed me two of her recent card acquisitions and asked me what I thought of them. I told her they were very nice and asked who they were for.

"That one's for Mary, and this one's for Rita," she said casually.

"Oh," I said, "I didn't know they were leaving."

"Neither do they yet," she said with a straight face. And with that, she returned the cards to the cabinet and lumbered off without another word. It was all very matter of fact.

Being calm was a rarity for Brenda because aggression featured heavily in her arsenal. Her caustic tongue and malignant rage were very much part of her DNA, as were her volatility and nucleotides. And yet, no matter what she did, her capital never diminished, and her behaviours largely went unchallenged. Very few staff members were converts to Brenda's management style, but most were conformists because they needed a job. She commanded fear in those who worked there, and she inhaled the fear she knew she'd instilled in others, and I think it fortified her. Other staff warned me about her early on, but it had to be experienced to be believed.

Brenda behaved as she pleased because she knew she could, and we all knew that no matter what she did, it was impossible to speak truth to power. Brenda did have an intellectual butler with whom she'd gauge some matters. Still, he was often conspicuous by his absence, especially when she'd been true to her brand and behaved particularly badly.

There was no genuine mechanism to handle a complaint impartially because she ensured that all complaints were triaged via her. This was tantamount to marking one's own homework and somewhat North

Korean in nature. So, because the staff were without agency, people just accepted it, knowing that while she would wound, she'd never kill, and they were almost grateful for that. This probably explained why, to use the football analogy, she seldom lost the dressing room.

Brenda chafed against all known conventions of how one may be expected to conduct oneself in the workplace. I quickly learned that bad language and inappropriate behaviour were fine just as long as they came from her.

I would often marvel at how she would berate one person for how they spoke to a colleague, and yet in the next breath, she'd be humiliating and insulting the very same person twice over. She'd then go on a tour around the office, stopping at different desks in different departments and telling everyone how individuals should and should not behave. I always felt that Brenda advising anyone on how to conduct oneself in the workplace was tantamount to the landlady of a rundown guest house giving hotelier tips to titans of the hospitality industry. Similarly, if you're going to criticise people for looking unkempt, don't do it with breakfast down your top.

From time to time, Brenda would suffer from a pang of conscience where she'd make an effort not to snap and snarl. When she knew she'd gone too far with what she'd said or done, she'd remind those who'd been on the receiving end of her acerbic comments or startling conduct how she'd gone out of her way for them. They'd receive a recap of her generous gestures, such as giving them a small loan until payday or turning a blind eye to something they had or hadn't done. Then, having planted these 'seeds' of aide-mémoires, individuals would then 'water them' with thanks and appreciation, and the germination of the cycle of further poor behaviour was cultivated.

Alas, Brenda's attempts to remain professional lasted about as long as a heavy smoker's efforts to quit smoking on New Year's Eve because just as soon as she received any kind of vaguely bad news, she'd revert to type. In fairness, her approach was effortless, and she conducted herself with the same casual ease most of us employ when switching on the kettle or brushing our teeth. For the most part, Brenda's behaviour was not a conscious decision; she'd done it for so long, it had come to define her.

On the plus side, it was cyclical, and you knew at some point it'd end as she'd move on to somebody else. It was almost Darwinian in that it was survival of the fittest and one became resigned to the fact that somebody was in for a tough time. However, the pill *was* sugared because if you'd had your turn, you knew it wasn't going to be you for a while. I'd hear people at the end of a 'cycle' say, "Oh, thank fuck she's moving on to somebody else now." It was a bit like when you've just had COVID-19; you know you're safe for a while and unlikely to be reinfected for some time.

When Brenda summoned someone, they were expected to go to her immediately, and if they didn't, she became pregnant with rage; in fact, by the time she finally got hold of the individual concerned, she was in her third trimester of fury. The truth of the matter was that Brenda struggled to get about the large and sprawling building due to her array of medical conditions, which she'd regularly list and overshare how many tablets she took a day to combat their impact on her beleaguered body.

The especially problematic condition was her prolapsed womb and we all knew a lot about that particular organ as we were updated almost daily regarding its whereabouts. She'd amble into a room and then announce, "Fucking hell, it's like having a dick between my legs." Then she'd shuffle off, bowlegged, to her next destination. Sometimes, I think it was said for dramatic effect, but other times, I think she was genuinely in pain and discomfort. Some would smile and nod at her announcement, while others, unwilling to enquire as to her well-being, would busy themselves with a task. If anyone did venture to ask if she was okay, she'd pull her hand out of her pocket, unclench her fist, give the V sign and say, "Are these yours?" as her magnified eyes didn't allow anybody to escape her gaze. And then she'd potter off, and this is why those in the know seldom rolled the dice.

As this was a solicitor's office, the law was practised daily, although there was a somewhat unorthodox approach to conventional employment practices.

The post of moral enforcer was vacant and had been for some time. It always baffled me how a firm that was horrified by the injustice some people faced, outraged by inequity and fought so fervently for clients' rights for very little remuneration, could have such a cavalier approach to how their staff were treated.

Survival could never be guaranteed, but you could significantly decrease your chances of being hit by verbal shrapnel if you expressed few opinions and kept your head down. Those with the greatest skill successfully managed to fathom the esoteric rules known to only a few. I didn't know the rules and never mastered them, so I tried to equip myself with a rhino hide resilience, but it was often porous, and I was cyclically wounded.

Brenda arrived early most mornings. She was audible before she was visible, as her car exhaust was lower than expected, compounded by all of the crew she used to ship in. They'd decant from the steamed-up car one by one, sleepy-eyed, yawning and stretching. This, in turn, incrementally relieved the road of the struggling exhaust, which must have been more prolapsed than Brenda's knackered womb. The passengers consisted of friends and family, and there was invariably some bickering during the drive in, on which Brenda would brutally adjudicate once the car had been relieved of its substantial load.

Some of the 'car people' weren't even dressed on occasion, and when this was the case, they'd traipse upstairs yawning and scratching and head for the shower. Remarkably, they weren't the only ones who'd use the shower either.

Now and again, Brenda would let a former client who was homeless and currently living in a nearby shed with his large, long-haired dog use the shower, too. I didn't half get a fright when I first encountered them on the stairs one morning. Occasionally, there was a queue for the bathroom, which you don't expect to see at a place of work where workers weren't engaged in manual labour, especially as not everyone in the queue was employed by the firm.

Knowing Brenda was to know that she was a staunch Christian. She had pictures of Our Lady adorning her tangerine-painted woodchip office walls with ornate rosary beads hanging off their frames. Not far from Mary was bottled water from Lourdes and miniature statues of Jesus smiling and holding out his hand, along with newspaper cuttings of modern miracles. There were even photographs of pieces of toast and plates of spaghetti which looked like Jesus both before and after he'd been on the cross. I hadn't encountered this before, but each to their own, I thought.

What I found remarkable was that Brenda's daily conduct was incompatible with the Holy Trinity's lessons of love and compassion. After much thought, I concluded that she must have assumed that having a lot of Christian paraphernalia on her walls would somehow afford her some credit with the big man or mitigate her poor behaviours.

Brenda's own office was not only at the heart of the mothership; it was where all important decisions were made, meetings took place and treaties were negotiated. There was a large 'Chief Prosecutor' sign wonkily sellotaped to the door, at the eye level of an extremely short person, which somewhat set the tone of the room's tenant. It was one of the most oppressive rooms I have ever entered. The room was searingly hot regardless of the weather, and the curtains never moved, no matter the time of day or year.

Entering the tiny room was also problematic, as the door wouldn't fully open due to a large upright metal filing cabinet behind it. So, you'd have to open the door as far as you could, then, upon a huge inspiration of breath, one could shuffle in sideways like a crab and stride over whatever files and paperwork had been abandoned on the carpet.

Stacks and stacks of files were on the floor, all piled on top of one another. These files had become resident and facilitated even more junk and carnage as further paperwork was being delicately balanced on their makeshift surface. The piles of paperwork on top of cabinets began to resemble a collection of Leaning Towers of Pisa, and it looked as though it was just a matter of time before they collapsed.

The mess which greeted you was phenomenal. When I first went in there, I thought it had been burgled; however, I soon realised that it was just in disarray. Brenda would spend countless hours in there, and to add insult to injury in a confined space, it wasn't out of the question for her to raise a bottom cheek and break wind with alarming gusto. Having lowered the aforementioned cheek, she would proceed with her task as if she'd undertaken nothing more than a routine throat clearance.

I had no idea what the surface of her desk looked like, as there was a layer three to four inches thick of loose papers and documents. This became a surface in its own right. She routinely assured everyone who entered that she knew where everything was on there because I think she knew it looked diabolical.

However, this chaos held real advantages for the foolhardy who hadn't completed something on time and were willing to take a gamble and play for high stakes. For example, those who were late with giving her something she'd growled for would wait for her to leave her office, creep in, stuff it under the paper mountain on her desk and creep out.

Such a strategy was fraught with danger, but if you were summoned, you could say, "Here it is" while pulling the item from the debris and tumbleweed inhabiting her orbit. This, of course, could be perilous, and you'd have to be extremely careful as to how you executed such a plan because if she thought for one moment you had got one over on her, she'd 'bank it' and you'd know about it within the next week or so. There could even be a leaving card bought for you in the cabinet.

Luckily for some, her memory was atrocious, and so occasionally, she'd forget that you were on her 'list' or your misdemeanours had been superseded by somebody else's, and so you might skip that particular cycle of maltreatment. Brenda's memory was so poor, she'd assigned different people in the office to remember her passwords for different things, because she couldn't remember them, and writing them down would only result in them being lost in Mount Paper.

Sometimes, she'd go into a room incandescent with fury and about to launch into some poor, unsuspecting person when she realised that she'd completely forgotten why she was annoyed and wanted to lambast them in the first instance. This then resulted in her being *even* more furious.

She'd occasionally return a few minutes later, having had her rage fortified by the indignity of forgetting what she wanted to say. Now, having remembered why she was livid, she'd launch a full-throttle diatribe of molten rage at someone. She didn't take them out of the room to conduct the one-way discussion; perhaps she was afraid she'd forget again, so she seized the moment while she remembered, despite there being an audience privy to the indignity.

On the other hand, she might have forgotten altogether and would have to accept that, and so to console herself, and while typing with one hand, she would delve into her voluminous bra, which must have closely resembled a baby's bonnet, rummage around and produce a warm, slightly moistened £10 note and then instruct somebody to go and buy her a large selection of chocolate bars. Fortunately, the confectionery haul usually pacified her.

As you might have anticipated, Brenda didn't take bad news well, which is perhaps why much of it got buried. Sometimes, it'd resurface, necessitating a minor miracle from one of the saints adorning her walls, and sometimes, it would never see the light of day again. Occasionally, it would have life breathed into it some months or even years later, by which time it had turned into a mammoth task, and the person responsible had been given one of the generic leaving cards, possibly accompanied by a clicky silver pen if they hadn't been too mutinous.

The majority of clients had used the firm's services for years, and she was incredibly well thought of by most and with good reason. She spoke to them with kindness and respect and always ensured they received the best possible service. I think it's fair to say that she bent over backwards for clients. This, however, meant that Brenda's chums largely consisted of gangsters and career villains, most of whom had a tendency to either die or spend decades residing at Her Majesty's pleasure.

Brenda always seemed surprised by their deaths, which surprised me, as I would have thought such a career choice would have come with anticipated health warnings of possible death as a near-certain occupational hazard. But die they did, and she was always absolutely heartbroken. Within no time, she'd have their photo added to the woodchip walls, wedged between the religious paraphernalia and iconography, and she'd draw everyone's attention to it as soon as they entered the room. However, her memory made it challenging to say anything remotely positive about the deceased after the third time. By the way she mourned their loss, you'd think we'd lost a national treasure or Nobel Prize winner, not someone who'd spent more time in prison than on the outside.

Occasionally, when one of her cronies was released from prison, they'd come into the office and visit her and those who'd worked on their case. These visitors had to be given very special attention, so much so you'd think we were receiving a celebrity A-lister, not a former category A, high-risk inmate. All work had to stop while everybody 'paid their respects'. This consisted of making them tea, shaking hands and backslapping. To be honest, I found it all a little incredulous. They'd done a ten-year stretch for something indefensible, not a ten-kilometre run for charity.

For those underwhelmed with criminality and unimpressed with what souvenirs or 'prison presents' could be smuggled out of jail, it was arduous and certainly tested my limited powers of small talk. I never knew what to say, so I masked. It's not as though I could say, "What have you been up to? It's good to put a face to the prison number." I just used to stand there with the people who knew what they should speak about and what faces to pull and try to make similar noises and gestures, all without looking too underwhelmed.

Although everyone knew Brenda wasn't legally qualified, nobody ever said anything as she'd sit in reception telling a client friend what she thought they should do. These legal training shortcomings were masked with sarcasm and facetious comments should anyone, even inadvertently, say anything to highlight her limited erudition.

Occasionally, Brenda would undertake file reviews and have experienced lawyers explaining their rationale to her, despite not always understanding the law or legal processes. Other times, she'd just leave a comment on the file which didn't bring any value to either the client or the progression of the case, and it was either ignored or met with a wry smile from those who knew better than to query its value.

Trying to explain a legal matter to Brenda would challenge the most accomplished of communicators, and what's more, the task necessitated serious diplomacy so as not to irk her. I'd hear others trying to explain things, and it was like watching a skilled potter craft a vase on a potter's rapid wheel, which could result in the clay going AWOL at any point with the slightest mishandling or poor choice of words.

This came about in part because she struggled with the complexities of the legal points, but more so because if she did not understand or disagreed with the statute, sentencing or, worse still, if she felt at all embarrassed by her own shortcomings or ineptitude, she'd adopt a particularly acidic means of letting you know what she thought of you and your explanation. This might involve snarling expletives through a curled lip two inches from your nose, while her clenched jaw failed to prevent her ill-fitting top denture from moving at a different rate to the words she spat out. As Brenda didn't appear to know how to professionally process the information, she was seldom realigned with accuracy by staff.

I remember the following broadcast being made and, just like in Hans Christian Andersen's book *The Emperor's New Clothes*, nobody said anything.

"Jordan has been to the court of appeal in London today on the Smith case. I am pleased to announce that the conviction has been squashed, which is good because he never did it anyway."

Nobody said there was no need to specify London. Nobody said it should have been "quashed" and not "squashed". And nobody commented on whether they thought he was or was not guilty, as that was not our concern.

If Brenda were to have known that staff were managing her, she'd have gone berserk. However, the savvy ones never let this be known, and that is, I later discovered, how they got through their day. They managed this febrile manager without the manager ever knowing that she was being managed. This was a skill I could only watch and admire, very much like a footballer who can score a goal from the halfway line.

Staff would come and go during my time there, which I think was a testament to the unedifying working environment. We had one person who lasted just eleven days, and some of those days were annual leave. The departing lady said she was more accustomed to working in an office where there was classical music playing, fresh flowers in the toilet and an altogether more cultured ambience. The only culture I ever found was growing up on the walls in the toilet and on the milk left floating in someone's breakfast bowl from last week under a pile of files.

Brenda's recruitment questions were interesting, too. She obviously knew that she swore a lot and had built a 'see how the land lies' question in her standard interview questions. Swearing was her number eight interview question. She stated that there was a lot of bad language in the office, and her question sought to ascertain if this would upset the prospective candidate.

If the candidate responded by confirming that they swore like a trooper, she was unimpressed and bordered on the judgemental. If they appeared to frown upon bad language, she'd claim that she wasn't sure how they'd fit in. Given that I only really ever heard her swear, I now know why it was included, although I'd have had it higher up the list than number eight.

It wasn't uncommon to find yourself in a 'dammed if you do – dammed if you don't' scenario with Brenda. Her dialogue was circuitous at the best of times, and it could be very difficult to ascertain what she was actually trying to articulate. She seldom spoke in proper sentences; there'd be no beginning, middle, end or 'take home message', and she'd sometimes just use random words that you'd be required to 'jigsaw together' to form some understanding. Where detail, specifics and precision were essential, invariably, none could be found in and amongst the threadbare conversation.

I often thought that if Brenda were to be provided with a verbatim written transcript of her dialogue, or even worse 'instructions', then perhaps she'd realise just how vacuous they were and, therefore, how difficult they were to follow. I say this because when she spoke to me, I wrote pretty much whatever she said down so I could go and re-read it; however, when I looked at my page after a 'conversation', it was just a series of mostly disconnected words, and so even though I had a copy of what was said, it was invariably meaningless.

Brenda's unique communication style wasn't because English wasn't her first language; it was because she just spoke in a nebulous manner and wasn't a great verbal communicator. Quite often, she'd forget what she was trying to say halfway through 'a sentence' or was distracted by somebody or something that necessitated her urgent intervention. Sometimes, she'd start to tell you something and then walk off halfway through, and you'd be left wondering, pen and paper in hand, if she was going to return or not, with no idea what you'd been left with.

If this were just one of her stories, that would be fine because no doubt it'd be recycled at a later date, as we'd all heard them countless times before. If you stuck around long enough, it was like a TV channel which regularly showed the same shows again and again within a short space of time. These stories came around with some frequency, as she'd completely forgotten about having told you the tale in the first instance, let alone the second or third time. I remembered them all, and I think others did too, as they'd smile and nod before the punchline we were all well versed in.

However, if she spoke to you with 'instructions', it was especially difficult, particularly for somebody neurodivergent. Some dyslexic people struggle with what's called 'working memory'. This relates to the ability to retain information in their head, even for a short period of time and even if that information has just been provided.

For example, if you were to be given an alarm entry code for access to a building, this may only consist of three or four digits, but if it's told to somebody with a poor working memory, they may struggle to 'hold' those numbers in their head, even for a few seconds. So, they may have to either write them down or input the numbers immediately. I've seen people with poor working memories 'hold onto' those numbers by saying them repeatedly out loud until they can write them down or input them.

Autistic people may seek clarity and require information to be presented in an accessible order or particular format. We may also need more time to absorb and process this information as our brains don't always take a direct route to the endpoint, as exemplified earlier on with my M8 motorway analogy. I require unambiguous language in bullet points.

Some people with attention difficulties may find it difficult to keep on task, focus on what they're being told and not become distracted, despite desperately trying to keep their mind on the matter. All of this should be considered along with the additional anxiety many of us neuro-divergents feel on a day-to-day basis, just trying to fit into and comply with the neurotypical world.

Therefore, to be tossed a few fragments of information for completing a task that most neurotypicals would find challenging was excruciating and super stressful. This was because I would invariably have to return to her and ask further questions or seek clarity on most, if not all, that had been belched at me.

Brenda didn't expect to have to say things more than once because, in her mind, she'd provided a perfectly adequate explanation, and either an individual had not been listening, or was being obtuse, and that individual was invariably me. Neither failure to listen nor being impertinent was ever the case. However, a combination of her oblique communiqué, Delphic instructions and my not having someone taking a bit of extra time to ensure I understood what was being asked of me resulted in my having no idea what was required or expected.

I know some of the 'normals' struggled, so imagine if you had additional needs. Most 'normals' were prone to just 'have a go' with what they'd be told and quite often got it wrong. This resulted in Brenda going berserk and informing everyone in the vicinity how it'd be easier to just "do it my fucking self". Never once did she think that her style of communication was at fault, and never once did anyone tell her.

Generally speaking, at this point, I could either take a chance and guess the way 'normals' did, or I could ask somebody else who might have overheard us and who was more 'fluent' in Brenda than me, or I could return to her for further decoding – the latter being the absolute last resort.

The term 'seeking clarification' was perhaps the safest phrase to deploy and I learned to use it often because it suggested that I'd grasped most of what was said, but I just needed to 'bottom out' a couple of points. It did not suggest that I needed her to start all over again and explain what she required of me logically and orderly, which did not require an intervention or translator.

Sometimes, I'd be left feeling that I'd just been tossed a few Egyptian hieroglyphics and left to get on with it without a translator's guide. There were numerous times when I'd have to return to her to 'seek clarification', as the combination of a smattering of words, a couple of shrugs and one or two hand gestures just didn't cut it and probably wouldn't have for most 'normals'.

I remember the first time I took a deep breath and returned to her, and predictably, she took it personally, as receiving bad news hadn't been catered for in her toolkit. Initially, she repeated the handful of words she'd originally uttered, but very loudly, deliberately and slowly, as a hearing person used to speak to a deaf person, or an English person may speak to a foreigner with broken English. However, seeing the blank look on my face, she took this for impudence. Unsure how to proceed, there was a 'Pinter pause' from a stony face as she decided her next move.

Having marinated in her white-hot rage for a moment or two, I was subjected to a prolonged delivery of the hairdryer treatment through disarming verbal aggression. I knew all I could do was endure it.

Expletives were being dropped during this almighty onslaught, her angry vein went into overdrive, and her face, whose features appeared vandalised, quickly went purple as it often did at the height of an episode.

However, as a toddler eventually wears themselves out after a tantrum, Brenda's momentum finally slowed down, and she sat back, smouldering after her emotional nosebleed. The scorched earth around her remained blistering for the rest of the afternoon, and I think she was probably radioactive for at least a day or so afterwards. I knew there was a good chance that a card would be bought for me sometime soon; however, in a few days, the typhoon had passed and was heading towards new waters.

During one of these types of episodes, the ADHD part of my temperament was on the cusp of challenging her treatment of me, protesting how unfair and unreasonable it was while trying to explain that all I needed was a bit of 'this' or 'that'. ADHD has a strong pull, and it can be difficult to rein in, especially when it comes to injustice. But the lucidity of autism soon placed a logical and unemotional hand on my shoulder, a foot on my verbal brake and steadied the rudder. While they're complete opposites, they often have each other's back.

There was no way of speaking reasonably to Brenda as I had as little agency as any other staff member there. She certainly had no bandwidth for reasonable dialogue, which may involve her conceding that she hadn't explained things clearly or that she'd verbally overstepped the mark. In all fairness, she had no terms of reference for her behaviours and management style as she wasn't challenged, and it was all she knew, so protestations would have been futile, not to mention imprudent, as any form of robust challenge could have resulted in a place having to be found for me on a witness protection programme. I soon learned that silently riding the wave was the only way out of a Brenda-based storm, but I didn't find it easy.

Of course, there are times when the logic and clear thinking of autism aren't always appreciated or apposite. I've been known to be very matter of fact and rational when pragmatism isn't necessarily in keeping with the mood, such as when somebody dies or is facing a life-changing event. At the same time, my ADHD hadn't done me any favours on these occasions either, because the words were often out before I'd had time to audit them or their impact.

As stated, there was no impartial means of complaining, and so nobody did, and Brenda knew this. Many people at this point would have left, but this was no ordinary job. Anybody who has ever tried to secure training in order to qualify as a solicitor will know just how difficult it is to get a firm to take you on. Not every firm is a training firm; some firms don't offer areas of work of interest to everybody, and competition for the small number of training places that firms have to offer has always been fierce.

There were, and I suspect still are, far more people looking for training contracts than places available. So, walking out wasn't an option, especially as I'd battled and put in more hours than anyone I knew just to pass the exams with a numeracy component. What's more, legal postgraduate courses aren't cheap; we are talking thousands of pounds, and having self-funded, I was mindful of the money I'd parted with. But above all, I refused to quit and so switched onto autopilot. It's not healthy, but it was necessary.

In any event, I was battle-scarred by the recent discovery of my learning shortfalls and the realisation that people with my smörgåsbord don't tend to get this far in life. They're either ruled out by society or an education system, or they haven't got the energy to fight the prejudices of the 'normals' and daily battles of the conditions.

I was also slowed down by the verbal wounds inflicted by Brenda and her lack of understanding around 'reasonable adjustments', along with the impact of her behaviours towards myself and others. Reasonable adjustments are things, changes or modifications that can be put in place for a person with a disability, which can make their life easier and a situation more accessible, and like a lot of disabled people, I need them.

That said, there was no way I was going to give up. I knew it was an unhealthy environment for me. However, I thought that as I'd overcome the exams containing numbers, the next part, as difficult as it was, was just a different kind of battle. I thought that, in a way, it was to be treated as 'time to be served'. I'd heard prison clients talk in this way, and I think there was something in it as a tactic to be adopted. I decided that this was going to have to be mind over matter. So, I devised a type of 'emotional dust cap' for my mentality.

This meant that not only would I have to mask on an industrial scale where possible, which would certainly drain me, but I would have to suppress my lifelong habit of being frank and speaking out against injustice. I hated thinking and behaving this way as it made me feel complicit and insincere, but I decided it was a tactic worth pursuing for the fixed time period of my employment. I needed to be more like the 'normals' to come out the other side. So that's what I did as best as I could. It wasn't without its own negative impact and emotional consequences on my mental health, but when I've set my mind to something, I won't fold.

When somebody is giving you a bollocking (deserved or otherwise), they expect you to look at them as a minimum. They want to know that their message is being delivered, and they need to feel that it's having the requisite impact. They do this by looking into your eyes because I think it fulfils some kind of human gauge of impact. This is difficult for autistic people, even in optimal circumstances, never mind gruelling or degrading ones.

Eye contact, for me, is bordering on painful and is as cringeworthy as being subjected to fingernails down a blackboard. Of course, in the neurotypical world, it's considered the 'done thing' to look at people when you're being spoken to, or speaking to somebody, even if you're not being hammered with a caustic tongue. It's what the 'normals' do. They look into one another's faces and focus on the eyes. This is as natural as breathing to them and gives them information about the other person's reaction and intentions. What's more, it also tells them if the message has hit home.

So, not complying with that human convention is conspicuous by its absence. As a result of poor eye contact, I have been accused of looking shifty, being disingenuous, not listening or being just plain rude. Whenever I try to explain my aversion to eye contact to somebody, I listen to my explanation. I find it difficult to make sense of it myself, so I understand why others may struggle with the notion that eye-to-eye contact is painful for us. Still, it absolutely is, and the 'normals' need to accept it and not try to rationalise or judge it.

I have tried over the years to make adjustments so that the 'normals' aren't so uncomfortable and unnerved by it. I've stared at foreheads or the nose, which isn't particularly easy. Other times, I've tried to walk or sit side by side with somebody as opposed to head-on; that way, I can 'mask' my discomfort and avoid the dreaded eyes, and the other person isn't expecting the return of eye contact while wondering why I'm looking everywhere but at them. As I've aged, I've taken to not bothering to put myself through the endurance of eye contact, and I'm hoping as awareness grows, so does understanding, and we don't have to put as many adjustments in place for the 'normals'.

When I was on the wrong side of Brenda's acid tongue, as painful as it was, I made myself look at her. It's what the 'normals' did, and I desperately needed to integrate. I was seldom successful because sometimes the laser effect of her eyes was just too potent, but I tried because I thought it might make me appear less perceptibly different. It didn't. I was always going to be the square peg living in a world of circular holes.

I wasn't alone in making adjustments for Brenda. While staff weren't always successful, they knew her 'triggers', and many were adept at avoiding them. They knew that everything, even the smallest of matters, such as where people sat or the movement of a desk, had to go via her. So, staff would do their utmost to reduce or remove the chance of her becoming belligerent or setting one of her angry veins off.

Engaging Brenda could be like a game which requires great manual dexterity, where each player needs to carefully remove a piece. If just one component is removed in the wrong way, the whole structure could come crashing down. Therefore, the knack was knowing how to extricate the piece you wanted, without disrupting the entire arrangement. Some staff had this down to a fine art, but I was far from being skilled in the craft, and would unwittingly remove the wrong piece at the wrong time. Sometimes, it was as though I'd removed a section while wearing giant foam hands, as the game's pieces could be strewn everywhere. This happened all too often, despite my masking in epic proportions.

Chapter 3
The Petri Dish

I can still remember my first day in the office. It was clear that nobody had thought about where I should sit, let alone where I would be working. When I walked in, I was greeted by an untidy reception desk occupied by two morose-looking lifeless pot plants, an old copy of a tabloid newspaper, a flickering lightbulb, and a well-thumbed catalogue with pages turned down on the gold jewellery section.

After some head scratching, pen top chewing and a routine emergency tea break, it was decided I should take 'Anne Frank's room', aptly named because of its diminutive size, hidden location and limited natural light. No special plaque adorned the entrance.

Upon closer inspection, it was clear that this unoccupied internal room, which cannot have been more than eight feet by six feet, was the unintended by-product of two ill-conceived other rooms; namely, it was the forgotten bit in between. The walls fell pitifully short of the saffron-tinged polystyrene ceiling tiles by around four inches, therefore partially compensating for the lack of any kind of window as one of the adjoining rooms had a window and donated some of its daylight first thing on a morning if the clouds didn't obscure the sun.

The room had probably once been painted white, but appeared to have housed a heavy smoker for a couple of decades. There was an untacked patch of muted carpet that had been arranged to cover most, but not all of the floor. The tiny space was barren except for an old wooden school chair and a small drop leaf table, which could only dream of having its wings spreadeagled. I don't know if there had ever been an old typewriter in there, but it wouldn't have looked out of place.

As I was becoming acquainted with my new environment, I could hear a strange noise coming from beyond the room, and so, with absolutely nothing to do, I decided to investigate.

As I left the room, I noticed a man outside the door. He had terrible teeth, even worse breath, a nervous twitch, a stammer, a limp and no concept of personal space. I asked if he was okay, but he didn't really answer, except for twitching a bit of a response with some coded facial tics. I found out later that Philip was one of the lawyers and throughout my time there, he could often be located lurking outside doorways for no apparent reason. I never did discover why; it was just something that happened.

I soon realised that the booming noise with an escalating glockenspiel warning sound was attached to a series of speakers. This megaphone system seemingly infiltrated every part of the large 1960s building. Every few minutes, it thundered and belched out messages, reminders and commands through the telephone speaker situated on every desk, in every room, as well as through wall speakers dotted around. This created more of a bustling train station ambience rather than an office environment conducive to concentrating and meeting clients.

It wouldn't be unusual for a loudspeaker announcement to start with something inane like, "Err…it's me…has anyone seen my red pen?"

Sometimes, the conveyer of the announcement would decide what they were going to say once the jingle had gone out to alert everyone that there was about to be an announcement; sometimes, they'd forget what they were going to say altogether or sometimes, they might just not fancy a trip around the building to look for their fag break pal and would megaphone them to save their legs and coordinate their meeting up.

"Black Donna to reception. Black Donna to reception…" or "Fat Kim to the back door. Fat Kim to the back door and bring your matches, babe."

I soon learned that few possessed good technique, so coupled with the frequency and prosaic nature of the announcements, I imagined that the PA system would become very taxing, very quickly. What's more, it was indiscriminate. Everybody always heard everything.

The combination of the speakers, the phones, the dictation of letters, the banter, the disputes and the conversations different people were holding with different clients over the phones was an absolute assault on my senses. It was like a noisy factory. I found it incredibly difficult for someone who needed routine and struggled with concentration, but I knew I needed to learn to adjust and adjust quickly. I had to watch the 'normals', follow suit and mask like hell.

I felt overwhelmed and overloaded, but I knew if I was to get through the next couple of years, I was going to have to learn how to switch off from it all. I bought some noise-cancelling headphones and did my best to limit the daily sensory intrusion from the 'factory floor'. It was by no means a fix, but it certainly helped circumvent the most distracting rhythms of the daily office commotion.

Young or old, nearly all the girls in the office smoked and smoked often. So as to avoid a nicotine-deprived stampede come 10:30 a.m., a strict 'fag 'n brew' rota was introduced and for the first few months at least, I think they adhered to it. The first batch would venture outside to draw the living daylights out of a strong foreign cigarette and the second batch would make the tea according to the wall list, which went something like this:

- Part-time Annie: Builder's tea
- Big Janice: Milky tea 4 ½ sugars
- White Donna: Black anything
- Black Donna: Black coffee
- Young Tracy: Tea colour of 2p

Part-time Annie was actually full-time but lazy. Big Janice was huge and only a few custard creams away from having to carry an insulin pen. White Donna was to be differentiated from Black Donna. Young Tracy was no longer that young but had worked there since she was very young and was still thought of as Young Tracy and so on. My name wasn't on the wall as I tended to make my own tea. I don't think I had a nickname, but if I did, I didn't know about it.

Due to the frequency of the inclement weather, the girls could invariably be located in the confines towards the back of the office. They'd be huddled together under a purpose-built corrugated canopy along with all the piled-up rubbish bags which were sometimes used as makeshift seats; that is, all bar Big Janice, who would have required a hydraulic hoist to get her back to her desk. There were times the back of the office resembled a junkyard but nobody seemed to care and it saved them from sitting on the rubbish bags, which had a propensity to smell like a warm Sunday afternoon at the tip during summer months.

I admired a lot of the secretaries and admin people I worked with. They took time to explain things to me and helped me settle in. They were down to earth, never minced their words and were fazed by nothing or nobody; they were all women and fine ones at that. Their sense of humour was quick and sharp and their one-liners were invariably delivered with a straight face and disarming accuracy. They'd share gossip and update one another on which lawyer had done what, whose inaudible dictation was getting on their nerves, or who was in trouble with Brenda and what she'd done.

Some months, you'd see a previously gold-cladded secretary with nothing left but the white marks betraying her spray tan where lots of chunky rings, bangles and necklaces were once worn with pride. Initially, I assumed that they'd forgotten to put them on, but after a while, I'd see that scrap gold envelopes were never far from view, particularly approaching payday.

Sometimes, I'd watch them on a lunch break, sitting there, chomping on chewing gum, full of orange fake tan and loads of gold, which may or may not end up getting weighed in towards payday, depending upon how much month was left at the end of a wage. Most of them had very loud voices and little need for an amplifier system, although it remained part of the daily humdrum.

On one occasion, one of the girls spent the best part of the week in chunky knee-high snow boots. She'd fallen asleep in front of an electric fire with all three bars full on after one too many alcopops and had managed to burn her calves. She didn't like the mottled look she'd been left with and dug out a pair. It was August, which did little to showcase the zeitgeist of this winter classic, but they appeared to do the trick. She must have been sweltering, but as with many unusual things that happened, nobody said anything, and I thought it wise to follow suit because, remember, I lived in their world.

I used to listen to their stories and remember one telling me about her being a WAG. I'm not a huge football fan, but nonetheless, I was impressed. I later discovered that her boyfriend played for the prison football team and not in a league as such; no wonder they laughed when I asked if she went to all the away matches.

One of the most memorable lines I ever heard was when the WAG told me how she was counting down the days until her boyfriend's release. I tried to show empathy and said how difficult it must have been for her. She conceded that it had been awful and then casually added, "My growler is chewing my leg off. I can't wait for him to get out." Although I have a propensity to take things literally, I knew this wasn't as it seemed and that her "growler", as she referred to it, was no animal, but then again, perhaps it was. Many of this hardcore collective had four interests: fun, fellas, fags and 'fangina' problems. And the 'normals' say that 'we' have a narrow range of interests.

It wasn't just fags which took place following a rota. Pretty much all refuelling and replenishing took place through a finely choreographed schedule and lunch was no exception. Needless to say, wages weren't lavish, but lunch was seldom brought in from home. Instead, the girls would copper up and frequent one of the many fast-food joints in the locality and buy something deep-fried with chips, the essence of which always clung to the air for the rest of the afternoon.

I think the dietary choices of some staff could, at least in part, have contributed to what I often had the misfortune to witness when walking past the toilet just after lunch. All I can say is that it sounded like a closely fought match point between two tennis legends, as the grunting became progressively virulent. Even when I had the foresight to arm myself with my noise-cancelling headphones, not even my trusted companions could prevent the auditory infiltration to which I found myself subjected. Sometimes it was even louder than what came through the speaker system.

I never worked out who was constipated nor responsible for ensuring that that toilet had to be abandoned for the rest of the day, but Brenda said, "There's a woman in this place who shits like a man." Given the poor diets of many, there were rich pickings and it was almost impossible to narrow it down.

Nonetheless, I had my suspicions. I recall one of the orange girls often walking around complaining of 'ring-sting' and another leaving the toilet in need of a senior member of the Catholic clergy to exorcise it. Moreover, no amount of a 'no frills' air freshener pumped into the vicinity could quell the acrid air. I concluded that there's only one smell worse than poo: floral poo. As the adage goes, you can't polish a turd.

While the smell was indeed noxious to anyone in possession of a nose and having the hardship of being in that part of the office, I understand it was particularly distressing for those still nursing last night's hangover, which wasn't uncommon. These poor souls had to find an alternative route through the building, but circumvent they did because to come within gagging distance of the 'ladies' (and I use that term loosely) toilets' would have left the most hardened boozers quite bilious from the olfactory experience.

That said, my pity was somewhat limited on the basis that as somebody with extremely heightened senses who can smell the common cold in my nose before its flourishing, this was truly shocking and I dreaded the afternoon bowel evacuations because I knew they'd squat in my nostrils until home time. Even the homeless ex-client who sometimes used the shower would try to use it before lunchtime so as to avoid that area and its pungent aroma.

One of the most endearing members of staff was a lady called Linda. When one of her emails came through, I, like others, stopped whatever I was doing to read it because they were guaranteed to be amusing and often shocking. She'd think nothing of insulting whoever had annoyed her, would warn them not to cross her again and was known to sign off, "You big baby, you!" Linda's understanding of email etiquette was to send everything to everyone, even if, as was often the case, she was only kicking off with one person.

Linda was a sturdy woman, built for comfort and took to wearing vests all year around due to her "time of life". Rain, hail or shine, she wore a vest. She even wore one to the Christmas party, except this one had glitter and sequins sewn on it. This fantastic woman who didn't give a toss was also in possession of a magnificently thunderous voice. She could bellow like an ogre and entered each and every room like a bailiff. Doors crashed open and she'd charge through, even when she wasn't in a rush. She was particularly determined if she was pursuing a lawyer, a breed known for their cavalier approach to work stationery supplies. Amongst her other roles, Linda had been tasked with being the gatekeeper of the stationery cupboard, and God help anyone she found "taking liberties" with her notebooks and pens.

Sometimes, Linda's daughter would covertly drop a baby off via the yard for her mum to mind while she ran some errands, and Linda would then strap this tiny little person to her chest in one of those baby hammocks and go about her business of charging through doors, shouting at people and undertaking missing stationery investigations. Remarkably, the baby never batted an eye. However, the bit that made me laugh was that she couldn't remember this baby's name and kept having to ask other staff members to remind her. I asked her why she couldn't remember this name in particular and she casually told me that she had so many grandchildren, all with ridiculous names, that it was hard to keep track.

While I loved listening to the girls chat, I thought I'd best be open with them about my aversion to social events and why. I've never taken to socialising, especially in large groups, and the thought of it makes my irritable bowel absolutely furious. I know socialising is loved by most, but I dislike and dread it intensely. I find it even more difficult to explain to bewildered 'normals' why I dislike what they love and look forward to so much.

Socialising people congregate in clusters, chatting about many things, most of which I don't like, don't do or don't understand, e.g., reality TV, shoes, lipstick, clothes shopping, etc. I am about as interested in these things as the Amish are in miniskirts and mankinis.

As for many autistics, unstructured times are excruciating and stressful. I don't know whom to talk to, how long I should talk for, what subjects are off limits or who best to avoid. I do, however, know there's usually a 'Queen Bee' character regarding groups of women. I usually manage to offend her with my honesty, and a version of events is then quickly disseminated to the rest of the hive, creating new problems.

Social events can be a strategic war zone, which is fine if you're well-versed in social combat and know how to dodge social bullets, swerve social grenades and scan for social land mines. But if you're autistic, you may struggle to undertake that vital and unspoken reconnaissance so many neurotypicals do when entering a room. The pitfalls are immeasurable and just the stress of having to put yourself through something pleasant for most, can often be a gruelling endurance test for someone autistic.

Having been regularly traumatised in a previous career by being conscripted to 'forced fun', I decided that I could no longer subject myself to social ordeals and be obliged to 'mask' and tell everyone what a great time I was having. 'Forced fun' was as bad as when a 'normal' is offended but claims to be 'fine'. So, early on, I spoke with Brenda when I knew a Christmas party was looming and tried to explain that I wouldn't be attending any social events along with my reasons.

Brenda looked at me aghast and so I tried to explain a bit further, along with the impact these events had on me, to which she said quite candidly, "Don't you think you're just being an ignorant cunt?" This was as appropriate as when she asked one of the girls who'd just been diagnosed with debilitating OCD if she'd like to clean her house for her.

Although I knew that verbal dexterity wasn't Brenda's strength, she wasn't alone in holding this view. I knew getting people to understand how difficult socialising was for me wasn't going to be easy because it flew in the face of what most people spent their week looking forward to, i.e., going out and seeing friends, etc.

I was especially glad I didn't have to attend that particular event because I later discovered that one of the girls got so drunk she couldn't be roused from the hotel foyer sofa. Evidently, the hotel staff were feeling for a pulse in her neck and placing mirrors by her mouth and nose to check for signs of breathing.

As I understand it, they were looking nervously at one another and then, just before an ambulance was called, she sprung back to life. She was fully rejuvenated after a power nap and clambered to her feet in some huge heels and a glittery top (still complete with drink stain all down it) and rejoined the dance floor with her tongue down somebody's throat in no time at all.

Chapter 4
Front of House

Those who drove through the area might casually glance over and see just a firm of solicitors. When I first drove through, that's all I saw. Little did I know that nestling near Dave-Downstairs, Shirley's Shoes, and an array of unusual eateries and bargain shops, I had an innocuous-looking Tardis of fascinating characters, extraordinary goings-on and remarkable situations before me.

Dave-Downstairs (aptly named because he was downstairs and some of us were upstairs) ran an extremely impressive 'Fag & Mags' shop further along the precinct, which opened when he woke up and closed when he'd had enough. It sold everything that any ordinary local shop might have to offer, except that it was extraordinary in that it was encapsulated in thick, bulletproof, bomb-proof glass and didn't have a known opening and closing time schedule attached anywhere. Following a spate of burglars seeking to relieve him of his wares, Dave-Downstairs had reverse-engineered the building, making it a fortress first and shop second.

Once in the shop, to your left and right, the thick glass and grilles allowed patrons to see everything. However, if they wanted any goods, they'd have to shout through a series of medieval arrow slits like the ones you see on castle battlements, and then the sound of the order would hopefully waft its way over, above and in between the rap, hip-hop, garage music and copious piles of scantily clad ladies showing off their wares in glossy top-shelf magazines.

If your request for whatever goods you'd asked for fell short and you hadn't been heard, you'd have to resort to either exaggerated mouthing like you were ineloquently trying to get your point across to people who are hard of hearing, or pointing your index finger on the glass so hard in frustration that the tip went white. If all else failed, you would have to ring Dave-Downstairs on his mobile via the handwritten number on a piece of torn-off card pressed up against the glass and talk to him on the phone less than two feet apart. I think I lip-read more than I heard when I did this.

Hopefully, if your order was received, your goods would be dispatched. However, they weren't dispensed ordinarily. A type of one-way drawbridge below the arrow slits was lowered upon which you'd place your money. This was then picked up, and your change, along with your goods, appeared from behind a series of sliding mechanisms as if quite by magic. Dave-Downstairs loved the security and, I suspect, would have invested in a moat if he could have got it passed by the council planning department.

Around the corner was an outlet called Shirley's Shoes, which I passed when going out for lunch. These shoes can only really be described as a display cabinet of crippling dominatrix-like footwear. Every pair was likely to give you at least a corn, if not a bunion and an unusual gait to your walk. When I first started working there, I just assumed that Shirley of Shirley's Shoes was on holiday or that I must have missed her opening and closing; however, some time down the line, I can honestly say that I never saw that shop open nor did I ever see any kind of stock rotation, let alone sight nor sound of Shirley. Testament to the inert movement of stock was the extensive sun damage to the 'shoes'. For example, a pair of once orange six-inch stilettos resembled a dried citrus fruit, and the purple dominatrix patent thigh-length boots were severely dehydrated.

There were many other fascinating organisations within the vicinity, too, including my favourite, an African eatery with only three dishes on the menu, all of which were lamb (or so I was told). However, they never had all three dishes available at once, so you'd usually be faced with a choice of two dishes, both of which involved lamb, chilli and onion. I adored eating there, and I wasn't bothered that I'd have to walk through the kitchen to get to the toilet, but my colleagues were less forgiving. Every time they knew I was going there to eat, I'd get comments that nobody had seen Dave-Downstairs' dog for a while, or did I ever wonder why I always had the whole place to myself. Undeterred, I kept on going.

The whole area was incredibly multicultural and diverse, and I thought it was magnificent. I marvelled at the smells of the different foods being cooked first thing in the morning, ready for the lunchtime trade, and sometimes I'd even try and pinpoint certain ingredients and components of the dishes, such is my heightened sense of smell and passion for cooking.

I thought that the African and Asian women in their colourful clothing all year round looked glorious. Although I never knew what music was being played, it always sounded like there was a wedding taking place, and I was in awe of the many different dialects and languages being spoken by so many different people. It was an exquisite sensory experience like no other.

For whatever reason, the experience was never a sensory assault, although it simultaneously activated all of my senses. During my life-time, I've been coerced into so many social and 'fun' events that they fill me with dread and anxiety even before I have arrived. However, this was different. I felt like an observer and was not forced to be a participant or mask. I wasn't expected to tell everyone what a great time I was having through gritted teeth, which was a huge relief.

If I had to say that there was a noise or sound that was totemic of my time in the office, I'd say it'd be police sirens, police helicopters and mini-motorbikes. Anybody who left a voicemail on somebody's phone or a welcome message on their answerphone would undoubtedly find a siren in the background because it was unavoidable as they were constant. From lunchtime onwards, mini-motorbikes could be heard zipping up and down the nearby roads, driven by unhelmeted kids. This, in turn, brought even more sirens out in force. Before long, the usual cat-and-mouse game started between the police and the motorbike rider, who often had his mate on the back, flicking Vs as the police chased them.

The clientele the firm served was eclectic. Some shared their woes on daytime TV shows, and others found solace in drugs or alcohol. Many had experienced hardship and troubled upbringings. Others knew nothing other than domestic violence and unhealthy family dynamics. Then there were some who were just unlucky enough to need our services.

None of our services were for nice things like seeking advice on a lucrative patent or a large financial inheritance. They were for the times in one's life when things were dire. Furthermore, not many of our clients could afford to pay for their legal advice and representation, so a fair few qualified for public funding. The lawyer applied for this; an official assessed the application, and the taxpayer paid for the services once approved.

Within a short period of time, I'd met such an assortment of people I realised how restricted my life up to that point had been. If I was told that the police wanted me and there was a warrant out for my arrest, I'd hand myself in immediately, quivering and shaking. However, one of the regulars told me to stop giving him grief about it every time he phoned because he was sick of me 'pecking at his head'. He then advised me that he did intend to hand himself in, just after his daughter's birthday party the following week. I found this kind of event planning wasn't as unusual as you may think.

There was one person who took pride of place in reception, and that was Denise. She could always be found there unless she was on remand in Brenda's room for one of her numerous misdemeanours.

Denise had protruding yellow teeth, cropped hair, a lacquered quiff and wore oodles of gold. She was a heavy smoker, shouted and swore a lot, barked orders and spoke incredibly quickly. She wore a long bobbly cardigan and a permanent frown. Denise was in a foul mood every morning, although I never knew why. She couldn't be spoken to until she'd had three fags, two cups of tea, and she'd exchanged her slip-ons for slippers.

She arrived every day on a moped or in an untaxed car, the latter of which still bore the scars from when she'd managed to relieve it of its last wheel clamp. The moped was parked near the front of the building, and you could tell by the way she resentfully dismounted that she didn't want to be there. When the local school kids got off the bus on an afternoon, it was seemingly far too tempting for some not to try and mount her bike, so she'd covertly stand sideways, peeping through a chink in the blinds surveying their every movement, like a caricature of your quintessential cold war Soviet spy.

As soon as one of them moved towards her scooter, she'd hurl back the blinds, take off her slipper and slam it against the window like she was swatting a big annoying wasp at the end of the summer season. When they looked up in surprise, she'd get her index finger and middle finger, point to her eyes and then point the same fingers toward them to let them know that she was watching them. They'd respond with the same two fingers, but used in quite a different manner. Having flicked the V sign, they'd run off, and Denise would return to briefing against whoever had annoyed her that day.

Her first job of the day was to ring up the clients due in court that morning to wake them up and remind them to attend. She'd tell some of them what to wear too if she knew them and thought they looked better in one outfit than another. Many were furious at being woken up 'so early', and she'd be greeted with a torrent of verbal abuse down the phone.

However, she was undeterred and just caught up on her emails, picked at a scab or tended to her cuticles, and ticked them off the list before disturbing the next one. Her view was that it'd save her a lot of time and hassle later on trying to find somebody to represent them at the police station when they were picked up subsequently by the police with a warrant for their arrest for failing to attend court if they had slept in.

Denise loved vicious-looking dogs and always had one as her screen-saver and a teddy version of the same breed of dog on her desk. She was regularly pranked as it'd go missing, only to be found hanging from a noose in one place or another around the building. On one occasion, she couldn't find it for some time and then started to receive a series of post-cards and ransom notes. Then, as if by magic, it reappeared.

Denise would think nothing of sharing her unsolicited views on Brenda and the way Brenda behaved with anyone within the vicinity. This included copious numbers of Brenda's friends and family who could be found in various roles in different departments at any one time. In doing so, Denise habitually overplayed her hand and was unceremoniously and quite brutally slapped back into shape by Brenda. Denise didn't seem to learn, saying that Brenda's rules changed daily and she'd usually give Denise just enough rope to hang herself.

Desperate for just an inch of power and authority, Denise regularly ran the gauntlet only to be subjected to Brenda's 'management style', which had been preserved in aspic from another era altogether. Denise's habitual quest for control enraged Brenda so much that there was a palpable force field around her following each of Denise's attempts to cement her position as Director of Paperclips or whatever role she was seeking to award herself that day.

What's more, Denise wasn't always immediately punished, so when she was, she didn't always see it coming. Watching Denise relentlessly chase power and influence was like watching someone turn their wage over to a bookie week in and week out, having bet on high odds horses each time, hoping for 'the big one', that life-changing win. However, in reality, all that happened was the odd small yield now and again and a mountain of debt and hardship.

When Denise's transgression was a serious one, or she'd said a little too much to one of the 'car people' or perhaps she'd ingratiated herself in an HR matter which had absolutely nothing to do with her, Brenda moved her into her office which devastated Denise. She was no longer 'front of house' and queen of all she surveyed. She was right under Brenda's nose being verbally abused, sniped at and oppressed, which caused her no end of problems, especially when her debt collector came to collect her weekly payment. Moreover, she couldn't keep a clandestine eye on her moped and often came out to lots of kids sitting on it, who liked to pretend to do wheelies, while making revving and roaring noises.

When Brenda was bored of terrorising Denise, or she'd forgotten altogether why she had moved her, she'd be relocated back downstairs. Denise would toe the line for a while, and the usual course of proceedings would resume. However, before long, Denise would have forgotten how awful it was with Brenda and would be back to her brazen self, smoking at the front door instead of at the back during her allotted time, being cocky, providing a commentary on anything that piqued her interest and so the process cycled once more. It was as predictable as night follows day.

Kelly was someone else who often could be located on reception, and

Denise considered her to be her sidekick. She wasn't, she just wasn't as loud or vocal.

What fascinated me was I couldn't believe Kelly was somebody's choice for front of house. She was the first person anybody saw (and smelt) when they arrived. Her thick orange foundation stopped cleanly around her jawline, so I have no idea how she always managed to get it all over the collar of her blouse. She had breath which could stop traffic, and if you'd put a canary on her desk, it would probably have passed away by the mid-morning fag break.

Kelly had short, stubby fingers and a constant head cold. She was utterly unperturbed when people openly told her that she smelt, needed a jet wash or advised that she might consider fumigating her clothes. The smell of old fags, fried food and dirty garments was engrained and almost engineered into the fabric of her clothing, and it was an odour which never shifted or altered from one day to the next. Frequent attempts were made to conceal it with cheap perfumes and air fresheners, but like floral poo, it was probably preferable in its original state rather than trying to disguise it as something else.

Kelly loved nothing more than to sit down at reception with an out-of-date copy of a criminal lawyers' reference book. She could spend an inordinate amount of time reading from that hefty book about what constituted different offences. When anybody passed her desk, she'd share an interesting fact she'd discovered that day.

She had a limited formal education after starting work at a young age. That said, Kelly possessed a keen and enquiring mind and would sit there working her stunted fingers through the pages, drinking it all in.

When somebody called in to see if the firm could represent them on a matter in the criminal courts, she'd say, "Wait there, let me get my *Bible* out." Then she'd sift through the well-thumbed pages with her nicotine-stained sturdy fingers, locate the offence and then look the person up and down to see if the crime suited their appearance.

Kelly was the front desk's doyenne of violent and sexual offending. A cornucopia of wisdom, if you will. If there was a defence, she'd know it. If you needed mitigation, she was your girl. Kelly could even tell you how long you could face behind bars if you were found guilty. Her knowledge was only limited to the age of the edition she'd managed to locate after its most recent confiscation.

Kelly had been told countless times not to refer to or dispense advice from her '*Bible*', be it from the new or antiquated copies, but she loved to delve into its pages and learn about offences. Perhaps she loved blue alcopops and cigarettes of a dubious origin a little bit more, but it was a close call.

Her favourite point of discussion was usually around 'intent', which holds its own particular legal significance. Few clients were interested in the semantics and most just wanted to be represented. When the text lost its appeal, Kelly went through a directory of barristers, noting interesting points about certain people and trying to establish which ones had been around the longest. To say this was a busy reception, you'd never have known.

I recall one day when I was in reception with a deaf client and their interpreter sorting out some paperwork. Kelly must have realised that she hadn't applied any deodorant that day or perhaps that it needed replenishing. So, without a second thought, she reached into her bag, took out a tin and liberally sprayed herself while sitting at her desk. Just at this time, another member of staff walked through reception to go out and said to her, "It'll take more than that!" and then left.

Kelly stuck two short sausage fingers up and told him to "Fuck off!" Just at that point, there was a knock at the entrance door by a man with a swarthy complexion and a huge Mexican moustache. While battling with a client on the phone, Denise leant over to Kelly, gestured towards the door and said, "Have you ordered a kebab, babe?" This was reasonable, as it was approaching lunchtime.

It turned out to be a client and not a food delivery. What made me chuckle, though, was that the whole scenario was being translated via sign language to my client, who, alongside the other client next to him with a parrot in a birdcage, was seemingly gripped by the ongoing dialogue and was following it in much the same way as spectators following a tennis ball at a hotly contested match.

Kelly and Denise were authentic and never did anything to hide their working-class roots, but that couldn't be said of everyone.

I have never understood people who are one thing and yet seek to portray another. I am also aware that there are some who don't know they're doing it. Some are insecure, some need to portray something else for a cause, some need to fit in, some are afraid of how they'll be perceived, or some are just ashamed of whatever it is they're trying to mask. I don't believe anybody should need to 'mask,' autistic or otherwise. Having people who are faithful to who they are seems to be an oddity in many circles. I squirm when I'm witness to disingenuity because I rely so heavily on authenticity to know what's real and what's a pitfall.

I saw 'working-class masking' played out a lot in legal practice, with people feeling the need to be seen as one thing or shoehorn themselves into another, and it'd usually start with the way somebody spoke. I used to listen to some lawyers dictate letters and attendance notes, and as soon as the microphone's red light clicked on, they almost became another person. It was as though they had developed a persona and needed to slot into it, just as a Shakespearean actor becomes that role once they grace the stage. However, they're nothing like Romeo, Juliet or Desdemona. The onset of the red recording light really could swiftly turn a Tracy into a Titania or a Mandy into a Macbeth, and I'd stare for a little bit too long sometimes as I was so shocked by the performance.

I remember whenever things had kicked off in reception, perhaps because someone had had a straightener, Brenda would sit in there at a desk for a few days to 'recalibrate' the atmosphere. When passing through, I'd listen to her answer the phones and direct calls and I'd be shocked at how her caustic and coarse tongue and regional accent had melted away, and she sounded more like a member of the aristocracy when they deploy the 'royal we'. However, as soon as the receiver went down, she was swearing and berating on a macro scale once more, with no regal residue whatsoever. The switch was seamless and similar to when a professional translator flips between two different languages.

Any pranks were reserved strictly for when Brenda was either out of the building or at least engrossed in somebody else's business. Occasionally, there'd be a stand-in on reception to cover holiday periods, and she wasn't as shrewd as the regulars, giving rise to countless entertainment opportunities. As soon as the pranksters realised she was in town, they'd concoct an antic that would amuse them.

Deirdre, the stand-in for Kelly, Denise or the other reception staff, took her role incredibly seriously. She would look forward to her *ad hoc* stints on the front desk, as she was a little underwhelmed with retirement and garden centres. Deirdre was a lovely woman, immaculately turned out and never swore. She was probably more suited to the 1940s war effort as a land girl and not dealing with 'kids' as she called anyone under forty.

Deirdre didn't like criminals, whether they'd been convicted or not. She was generally unhelpful to clients seeking legal advice on criminal matters, and if they called from prison, she thought that they must be guilty, and so was even less helpful. I don't think she knew that those on remand hadn't been convicted of anything at that point.

Her favourite clients were those seeking a divorce or the mentally ill. She liked these clients because they'd done "nothing wrong". Such was her disdain for the criminal law clients; if somebody walked in off the street and asked if we could do a retraction statement or a bailed client came in on a very serious Crown Court matter and wanted to transfer to us, she'd just say, busying herself with some innocuous task, "I'm sorry. We don't do crime."

Although many areas of legal work were undertaken, criminal cases were a significant part of the firm's work, and so being told that we "didn't do crime" when everyone knew we did was like somebody walking into a supermarket and being told that they didn't sell bread or tea bags.

Exasperated but amused by Deirdre, it was decided it was time for some fun. One of the lawyers called in off a blocked number and decided to assume the guise of the lowest of the low – a client in prison. Realising that the call might be from a prison as the number was blocked, Deirdre let out a long, slow sigh and commenced her prepared patter of the firm's name, her own details, and her offer of 'help' whenever she answered and went into autopilot.

The conversation went something like this:

DEIRDRE: Good morning, (name of the firm), Deirdre speaking. How may I help?

CALLER: Hiya. My name's Peter. I'm after help for my next parole hearing to get released. Can you help me? I'm having my human rights abused. It's double jeopardy and it's not on. I'm being pushed from pillow to post here and have had enough. I want to get my sentence squashed because keeping me locked up like an animal isn't on.

DEIRDRE: Okay. What's your name?

CALLER: Peter. Peter Sutcliffe.

DEIRDRE: Can you come into the office?

CALLER: No. I'm locked up, and they won't let me out.

DEIRDRE: Do you get day release?

CALLER: No, they don't trust me.

DEIRDRE: Ah, that's a shame. I'll just take a few details so I can pass them on.

CALLER: I want a hearing. I'm fed up with being stuck in here; it's a shithole, and there's nowt to do. They've taken the satellite TV down. I'm only allowed the games console twice a week, and they won't let us have any more of those Thai brides sent in. And the sweetshop won't stock chocolate finger biscuits anymore. I've had it, and I want out. I need to get out before I do something silly.

DEIRDRE: Okay. I've got all that down. What's your name again?

The caller honed their best Yorkshire accent and deployed a few choice phrases often used by clients into the mix for authenticity, so the conversation progressed. Never once did Deirdre twig that she'd been 'speaking' to a notorious serial killer and duly sent the referral on to the appropriate lawyer (minus a surname).

Thrilled with the success of the first jaunt and undeterred by the consequences of getting caught by Brenda, a second prank was concocted some hours later.

DEIRDRE: Good morning, (name of the firm), Deirdre speaking. How may I help?

CALLER: Good morning. I'd like a divorce. I've had enough. I can't go on like this anymore. I'm at the end of my rope.

DEIRDRE: Okay, my love, what's your name?

CALLER: It's Anne.

DEIRDRE: And what's been going on, my darling? Tell me all about it (as she settled into her seat and started sipping her tea from a China cup and saucer she'd brought from home, while starting her second chocolate biscuit and dabbing the crumbs from the corner of her mouth).

CALLER: (All tearful and full of snot bubbles) I'm fed up. It's all hunting, wrestling, jousting and birds, hawks in particular, and don't get me started on all the other women. I don't get a look in anymore. And he's really let himself go recently.

DEIRDRE: (Fishing for the more salacious details) They're all the same, my love. I had forty-seven years of it. So, what went on then? You know, just so I've got something for the form.

Despite later asking for a surname and having been given the name of Boleyn (once she'd extracted a plethora of sordid details), Deirdre still had no idea that she'd 'spoken' to the second wife of King Henry VIII, from the sixteenth century, notorious for uxoricide. She dutifully completed the form, offered a bit of marriage advice, imparted some of her own experiences, probably from around the time of the Blitz, and sent 'Anne' on her way feeling much more positive.

Meanwhile, the caller was thrilled with their plummy accent, and the crowd of people hanging around the phone elsewhere in the building listening in were delighted at the success of the calls. I have to say, if anyone doubted Deirdre's view on criminals compared to divorcees, then listening to her speak with 'Anne' compared to 'Peter' would leave them in no doubt.

Pranks and antics were a regular occurrence, and the speaker system often played a key role in their execution. The word 'gate' is often attached to scandals in the media and equally, it came to be used whenever there was a period typified by investigation, controversy, scandal and conspiracy theories in the office. The most notorious for us was 'Speakergate'. It started as a bit of a joke, with people making comical statements. However, like most things, it promptly went downhill. Before long, there was burping, farting, impersonations, an order for Indian takeaway and general rudeness in foreign accents coming through. Goodness knows what clients in the interview rooms must have thought, as there were phones with loudspeakers in those, too. Brenda walked in during the shenanigans and stood there listening, simmering and luminescent with anger.

People were called in and interrogated. There was speculation as to who had done what and suggestions as to what would happen to X or Y. Brenda never did get to the bottom of who was involved, thankfully. I suppose it's difficult to identify the culprit from the sound of a fart, babblings in a foreign accent or rantings in a broad Birmingham accent ordering a takeaway.

Every day there was like sitting on a bucking bronco on full throttle, with my main objective being just to hold on. Some were undoubtedly better at it than others, and all were better at it than me. The more experienced even managed to enjoy the ride, but as a novice, I found each day took me through a gamut of emotions. But over time, I went from being wobbly and falling off a lot to managing to remount with a modicum of dignity and getting better each time.

Chapter 5
Crime

When I trained to be a solicitor, I was required to undertake a number of 'seats' or areas of experience. Each seat was to be supervised by an experienced solicitor. This meant that I had to work in different legal departments to gather a range of experience and knowledge to qualify as a solicitor.

My first seat was criminal defence work. I wasn't told what work I'd be undertaking or what was expected of me other than I'd be "working in crime". This is all I knew right up to when I walked into the criminal department and said, "Hello!" to my new colleagues.

Nebulous as ever, I found Brenda's lack of direction and absence of detail extremely difficult to manage because being able to prepare myself was (and still is) a vital coping strategy. I don't expect to know everything in advance. However, enough information to anticipate events and manage my expectations makes a huge difference. For many autistics, the unknown is difficult to countenance and causes me, in particular, incredibly high levels of physical and mental anxiety.

Nonetheless, I was going to have to get used to incomplete instructions and ambiguous communication because having the audacity to ask Brenda for any timetable or detail about what I was supposed to be doing resulted in my being verbally pummelled with facetious comments inches from my face.

"Do you think I've got nothing better to do all day than sit and fucking think about you?" This was Brenda's response to my query about what I might be doing in this seat.

I didn't want to occupy her day. Just a cursory thought would have helped in the first instance, and it wasn't unreasonable.

This was a heavily deployed tactic by Brenda when she didn't want to concede that little to no thought had been afforded to something which should have been afforded due attention and consideration. In my case, it was my training, supervision and any kind of 'reasonable adjustments'. It's not like I hadn't been open from the start about my conditions, so I have no idea what she thought constituted 'reasonable adjustments', let alone professionalism in the workplace.

Although this was ableism at its gilt-edged finest, I was also aware that I wasn't being singled out and that none of the other trainees were told any more than I was. I assumed they'd been wise enough not to ask. However, having a bit of time to prepare was such an important adjustment for me, and it was noteworthy by its absence because my anxiety skyrocketed.

When I don't have time to prepare and things are just sprung on me, my stomach feels as though it's dropped, just as the participants of a rollercoaster ride feel when it starts its vertical descent from a great height. Or perhaps when an aeroplane encounters turbulence and many passengers know their insides momentarily feel strange due to sudden altitude changes.

Then comes the follow-up. Crippling anxiety is something I've lived with all of my life. Once the stomach has dropped, I'd liken the ascent of my anxiety to what happens when a brawny participant has taken up the challenge at a fairground to the call, "Step right up!" to the 'High Striker' or 'Strongman Game'. Once the lever has been struck by the mallet with sufficient force, the puck will shoot up the shaft, and once it reaches the top, it'll ring a bell. My anxiety surge works in much the same way, and the bell was sometimes rung more often than I could cope with during my time there.

When I first started "working in crime", I was directed to a shelf with loads of paper files of varying thicknesses and told they were all mine. Far from being grateful, I looked at the overwhelming number of files on the groaning shelves and had no idea what I was supposed to be doing with them. I also knew they'd all be time sensitive and I needed to get to grips with them quickly, but I had no idea how to do it.

There was no instruction manual or even handover note from the last trainee who'd previously been in that seat, and nobody provided me with any kind of meeting to say what was required. Brenda had introduced me to a couple of criminal lawyers, which was preceded by her telling me not to make a "fucking nuisance" of myself by asking too many questions, as it was a busy department. So, with Brenda's "working in crime" induction complete, I was left to it.

I pulled the files out one by one, and although I didn't really know what I was looking for, I thought I'd try and see how the older and fatter ones had been put together and worked on; that way, I might be able to 'reverse engineer' my own files.

Many lawyers made themselves known to me pretty quickly, primarily because they wanted their preparation and work undertaken first. I saw this as a means to find out what I was supposed to be doing and told them that I'd do whatever they needed me to do; all I needed was a bullet point 'shopping list', and that, I have to say, worked a treat.

The 'shopping list' is called a 'Case Plan' in the legal profession, and I undertook whatever task they'd put on there. One of the lawyers who was resistant to this once wrote, "Please take a view of the attached documents and then let me know." I had no idea what he was talking about and what he wanted from me, so I let him know that asking me to "take a view" was wholly insufficient. Needless to say, his work wasn't completed until he told me what he wanted – properly.

So, if it was vague or not on the shopping list, it didn't get done, although if I was unclear about what they wanted, I always asked them.

This was a lesson for them, too, insofar as not making assumptions or being lazy regarding instructions. If I hadn't done something that they wanted, they soon learned, having had their attention drawn to their own incomplete shopping list. I used to remind them that they wouldn't send someone shopping and berate them for forgetting the milk if it wasn't on the list.

Some were a little resistant, let's say, when it came to the list. Nonetheless, I persisted, and they eventually acquiesced. I decided that I needed to be vocal on this matter because it was a deal breaker in terms of my doing a proper job for them. They wanted things done properly, and I wanted to do a good job, so we needed to go on this journey together to some extent. I think they may have spoken about me and decided that I meant business, which I did. While I may have been new to legal practice, I knew my request wasn't unreasonable.

Each lawyer got used to writing the 'shopping list' for me. Although there were some commonalities in each file, there were invariably numerous unique aspects, too, depending upon the case's merits. So, I'd do things like write to the Crown Prosecution Service (CPS) who were conducting the prosecution and obtain information from them pertaining to their evidence against our client. When it arrived, I'd work through the bundle of documents, CCTV, interviews and statements. I'd listen to the police interviews, look at witness statements and take statements from our clients, based on their account of events, which tended to differ from the police's account of events. Sometimes I'd have to watch CCTV footage too, if it was being relied upon, and then see what the client had to say about it when we watched it together.

All criminal cases start in the Magistrates' Court, whether somebody is being prosecuted for stealing a loaf of bread or murder. If the offence is the former, that's where it's likely to remain. However, if it's more serious, the magistrates will essentially send it up to the Crown Court, as magistrates have insufficient sentencing powers to deal with the matter. So, I was involved with a variety of different cases because I was predominately dealing with cases at the beginning of their life cycle. Some were more serious than others, but many passed through me in the first instance to get them ready for court.

When the lawyers specialising in criminal law attended the Magistrates Court and the list of cases was particularly lengthy, I was sent to help as a 'runner', and I loved it. It was frenetic and fast but a great way to learn and see the law in action. I'd collect the paperwork from the prosecution bringing the case to court, convey messages where necessary, take instructions and complete funding applications if a client had been picked up on the duty rota the night before. This rota is where different firms provide police station advisers, who are available out of hours on a rota scheme, should somebody who has been arrested require legal advice at the police station.

This was all while keeping in touch with Brenda, who had some trust issues and thought everybody must be sitting around, drinking coffee and chatting. She regularly wanted to know exactly what was happening and when we'd be back.

Now and again, I was sent to the Crown Court to sit behind the barrister and take notes for the instructing solicitor back at the office. It could be frustrating to see clients who appeared to go out of their way to give the worst possible impression to a judge and jury. I remember one occasion when the judge asked the defendant if he wanted to stand or sit, and he elected to slouch. However, what happened next I hadn't seen before.

The client sat there for the entire time, with his hands down the front of his tracksuit bottoms and stared at the jury in the most malevolent and menacing manner possible. Then, just as I thought that he couldn't endear himself any less, without invitation, he shouted across the court and told one of the members of the jury to stop giving him "fucking evils", and this was then followed by a barrage of swearing, shouting and abuse to the other eleven members. He had to be removed by security, kicking and screaming.

However, for the most part, I was office based and had contact with various clients. Working in the office meant that clients came in to see me, and in that sense, they became very much part of my daily routine and the wider office environment. Many clients knew the staff, and some of the regulars knew the staff really well as they'd all grown up in the same area. Clients were very au fait with the office, and there was a warm dynamic between clients and staff.

I began to be decreasingly surprised that entire families with kids in buggies full of piss and biscuits would rock up to the office, complete with a dog on a string. Regardless of the entourage they brought with them, I'd have to go through statements, view CCTV and take instructions from them, which wasn't easy because there could be many people in a small room.

Some clients would insist on the whole family joining them in the office interview rooms, which consisted of a small table and two chairs.

This meant it was standing room only for the wider family, but pour in they did. Despite being crammed into a tiny space, extended families were undeterred at being vacuum-packed and rammed into a minuscule area, only big enough for a long-forgotten and extinct tribe of tiny humans. There was no scope to step in any direction but this didn't deter anyone.

Despite there being standing room only, they made good use of their time by undertaking such tasks as rolling fags, texting mates or something which many seemed to love – eating pasties. Most clients I dealt with had a serious pasty habit and would think nothing of covering the floor with debris from their and their children's pasties or jumbo sausage rolls eaten from the paper bag.

The only time a pasty was put down was when the person sitting at the table with me changed a nappy. As soon as that task had been completed, pasty consumption was promptly resumed, and no hands were washed or sanitised. I was always exhausted by the en masse family gatherings and was relieved when they were over despite the room being devasted. On one occasion, I was handed a warm and filled nappy in a carrier bag to dispose of following their departure. I'm still not over that.

One of the first cases I was involved with concerned the practice of Voodoo. Despite years of legal study, witchcraft, sorcery and black magic were new to me. I was asked to take instructions from this client, which involved asking him questions about the allegation, taking his account of events and allowing him to put forward the information he wanted to present when the matter went to court.

The gentleman sat across from me and stared at me with an unfamiliar intensity. Even if I'd have wanted to make eye contact with him, I don't think I could have, as his gaze was so consuming. Our client was seeking to have the practice of witchcraft form part of his defence, on the basis that he had been subjected to its undue influence because he'd had spells cast upon him by a witch doctor.

Manifestations ranged from disembodied footsteps heard around the house to his wife suffering fertility problems, which the pastor back in the Caribbean had explained resulted from a negative entity having been lodged in her womb. The same entities would visit the couple during the night while they were sleeping, leaving them exhausted, drained and covered in marks on their bodies. The curse was also responsible for him being exposed to unprovoked attacks from strangers he told me. Seemingly, the jinx had impacted all aspects of his life.

For the first time, I felt really uncomfortable taking instructions from a client in the office and wasn't at all consoled by his assurance that the silver chain I wore around my neck was a good source of protection. He went on to inform me that anyone attending court needed protection too, although, despite my probing, I didn't manage to establish exactly what kind of protection was required, but nonetheless added it to my 'shopping list'. At the same time, he told me that the number three must be avoided at all costs, as it had sinister connotations. I noted all of this down and passed it on to the solicitor with conduct of the case. Many of my colleagues dismissed him and his warning of the calamitous portent as nonsense, and I don't know if they were right to or not, but I did hear that in Court Three at three o'clock, he was found guilty.

We had a lot of clients who were returning customers, such was the frequency of their offending. I recall one of the lawyers coming in and being rattled about one of our regulars. She came in and said, "He's off the fucking scale. He's going down for this one. He's getting potted." This is something I heard on a regular basis, so I didn't take too much notice.

However, when I listened to the police interview, I knew why. He had been arrested on yet another very serious matter, and while in the police van, he performed what is sometimes termed a 'dirty protest'. To the uninitiated, this means protestations using one's own poo. He was accused of smearing excrement all over the inside of the police van.

The interview about the initial matter and dirty protest never really got underway because every time a police officer showed him a photograph of the van and the carnage he was alleged to have left, he'd tell them it wasn't poo because it was "rust" or "dirt". The only poo he'd done was a "neat little one in the corner", and he'd left it all nice and tidy otherwise. He didn't want to poo in the police van, but he was desperate and had no choice, according to his account.

The entire interview was a discussion about the difference in colour between poo, rust and dirt. The interview also kept having to be stopped as the smell was too overwhelming for all concerned in the police station interview room. The gagging noises were audible over the recording, as the pernicious odour had clearly clung to our client.

I couldn't smell the poo or "rust" over the recording, but my acute sense of smell went into overdrive because I knew exactly what it must have smelt like: the women's toilet after the "woman who shits like a man" had parted with her post-lunch load. At that point, any sympathy for those in the police interview dwindled. I had to put up with evil poos, floral poos, Indian takeaway poos, night out on the tiles poos, anxious poos and poorly poos, Monday to Friday. This, unfortunately, wasn't my last encounter with dirty protests.

One of my first deployments while "working in crime" was to a prison to take instructions from a client. I'd never been to a prison before, so I was curious and unsure what to expect.

In the waiting area were children's toys and picture books, which I hadn't envisaged. On the first occasion I went, it must have been a day for family visits as well as legal visits. I remember seeing a couple of toddlers wearing gold identity chains and bracelets, squaring up to one another and having a straightener over a toy they both had laid claim to. Neither of them were backing down. Meanwhile, their immaculately turned-out mothers, with pristine hair and makeup, prepared to see their loved ones and were applying the final touches to their flawless lipstick.

Having checked in at reception, we all went through security one by one. As an adult, I was unfamiliar with the process; however, some toddlers could have easily explained it to me. When it came to being searched, they were all clearly well versed in the practice and stood there expectantly with their arms apart and legs astride and evidently thought nothing of being frisked and putting their shoes through a machine.

Having gone through the airport-like security, I found myself alone in a small, very thick, bullet/bomb-proof glass 'security capsule'. It was security at a level Dave-Downstairs could only have dreamt of. This enabled me to progress to the next part of the prison. I'm not sure what happened, but as one door closed, the other didn't open, and I was trapped in a glass box.

No amount of knocking and banging brought me to the attention of any official. I must have looked desperate in there: troubled face, eyes like saucers, mouthing while my clammy palms were pressed against the glass. I must have resembled the French mime artist Marcel Marceau. Eventually, I was spotted and released. I'm sure I wasn't in this holding cell for long, but it seemed like an eternity as I watched the world go by, and all those around me were seemingly oblivious to my inaudible pleas and knocks.

Naively, I was shocked to discover how many of our clients from all the different areas in which we practised were illiterate, and clients in prison seemed to struggle more than most. I soon learned to be especially mindful when writing to them that I needed to explain things in a super accessible way, but without losing content or being patronising. I was also aware that some of them would enlist the help of a trusted friend to read to them aloud so they could understand the substance of the communication.

When I started learning the law, I knew I was going to have to be able to explain legal matters to many different types of people from different walks of life. However, I didn't anticipate having to write and explain matters in such simple terms on occasion, without being reductive. Nevertheless, I enjoyed this aspect of the job and wish more time had been dedicated to preparing me for such realities at law school.

Like many, I assumed that literacy was just a given, but poor reading and writing isn't something people boast about, so I guess it's seriously underestimated. Also, since my diagnosis, I had benefitted from and appreciated people taking extra time with me to explain things I struggled with. I knew how important and empowering it was for me to return the goodwill, and seeing the difference it made to some people was wonderful. Whether some hadn't been to school much or had learning needs, I don't know.

Around this time, Brenda had decided to be preoccupied with tidiness and orderliness. As I was in the office for much of the time, I witnessed this temporary but intense interest. It was a bit like a special interest, except that it didn't bring her or anyone else joy. Nobody knew where the rationale came from, but it preoccupied much of her day and ensured that the mountain of paper on her groaning desk grew even higher. This quest involved 'encouraging' people to be neater despite still living in an office full of landfill and pastry debris herself.

She'd walk around the office like a high-ranking official inspecting the troops and assessing everyone's workspace, which might involve aimlessly pushing piles of paper around on someone's desk. She'd also use phrases like 'health and safety' without any context or meaning.

However, in true Brenda style, 'Operation Shit-Tip' was managed with all the appositeness and diplomacy one might imagine. She'd walk around the office being obnoxious and acidic. Or, while staff were out, leaving large handwritten notes in marker pen taped to their computer screen, delivering such messages upon their return as "*Get this shit sorted. Brenda*" or "*See me. Brenda*".

Where I would sit in the office would be determined by the work I undertook. For a while, when I was "working in crime", I was seated next to a tiny man called Jeffrey. If he didn't qualify as having a condition, he couldn't have been far off. Jeffrey was particularly chaotic and disorganised and was therefore targeted by Brenda when she was implementing her new office sanitation regime.

For some reason, which I never quite got to the bottom of, Jeffrey would bring his clothes to work. He'd then change there, but wouldn't take the worn clothes home. At the end of some weeks, he had what can only be described as a 'floordrobe' around his desk. I remember coming in one morning and thinking how it looked like a changing room at a children's outfitter specialising in formal attire, with numerous tiny outfits and miniature waistcoats strewn everywhere.

Jeffrey would graze on brittle food all day long, which would shower his desk with food rubble. When I was away from my immaculate workspace, probably with a large family gnawing their way through crumbly pastries in a confined space, I'd come back to find that he'd moved onto my desk, with a new range of brittle food and no invitation to be there. This desecrated my keyboard with thousands of crumbs and violated my spotless and fastidiously arranged area. To add insult to injury, he'd change all the settings on my computer and adjust my chair so that it was just about the right height for a Pygmy person.

Jeffrey was untidy by the standards of most. Still, for someone autistic who needed order and continuity, particularly in a tumultuous working environment, he was quite possibly one of the worst people to be within a two-mile radius of.

As I was "working in crime", my contact with Denise in reception inevitably increased. I think through a combination of smoking and shouting, Denise would regularly lose her gravelly voice, which I have to say came as a great relief to all concerned, especially the criminal clients whom she'd routinely wake up first thing in the morning.

Denise saw a trainee lawyer as an opportunity to exert herself and would inform me of things such as where she expected me to be in terms of my funding form completion abilities, which would enable clients to have their cases funded by the public purse if deemed eligible. Depending upon where she was in the cycle of being subjugated by Brenda, she'd also test the water by making capricious demands, such as instructing me to deliver her printing from the nearby machine, although I'm unsure how her larynx affected her legs.

So, to make herself understood at reception or assign Kelly tasks she had no authority to, Denise took to 'aeroplaning' messages written on bits of A4 paper to her sidekick, who didn't appreciate having her time with her *Bible*, playing on the internet or talking dirty to her latest boyfriend on the phone interrupted. Although she occasionally opened the note, Kelly often just 'aeroplaned' the message back without reading it, particularly if one of her distractions had reached a critical juncture.

Seemingly, the loss of Denise's voice also necessitated extra-long lunch breaks, which I later discovered were to enable her to go home and have sex with her husband. As it gave everyone peace, nobody said anything and they even covered for her. On occasion, when Brenda was bashing out loudspeaker demands to locate Denise, excuses would be made, knowing that it was unlikely that Brenda would venture around the building looking for her as she'd have to drag her womb with her.

"Working in crime" also ensured I saw more of Linda and the inside of her prized stationery cupboard. Linda fascinated me and was a law unto herself regarding holidays and time off. Just like other staff members, Linda booked her annual leave as usual; however, she seldom returned when anticipated. Before being *au fait* with this particular idiosyncrasy of Linda's, I remember looking for her on her supposed first day back and being told she might not be actually 'back' until the following week or perhaps the week after that. Seemingly, it was difficult to predict.

If Linda was having a good time on holiday, which she usually did, she would think nothing of returning when she fancied as opposed to when she said she would. So, two weeks of leave could turn into a month long or so. When Linda finally returned to the office, she acted like it was normal. To be fair, it had become the norm for all concerned.

Linda was lambasted by Brenda every time, but it didn't make the slightest bit of difference. On one particular episode of Brenda's HR spillages, she revealed to all within the vicinity that Linda thought that 'holiday' was just when you were actually out of the country, for example, on the beach, perhaps with a cocktail after applying some Factor 30 suntan lotion. Therefore, if she went on holiday for two weeks and then spent two weeks at home recovering, that was two weeks' leave, not four. I don't know whether Linda didn't grasp the concept of annual leave or Brenda's oblique turn of phrase had just fallen short of a satisfactory explanation. Nevertheless, still not grasping the annual leave rules, Brenda called Linda's annual leave "out of the office time" to avoid confusion and extended periods of unauthorised absence.

It wasn't just "out of the office time" to which Linda applied her own rules. On occasion, when she fancied an impromptu day off work, she'd ring in on the day, not long before opening, to let everyone know. Having utilised more of her "out of the office time" than anticipated, Linda would phone in and leave a message on the answering machine. Unfortunately, she seldom planned the reason for her 'sickie' and would think of and then cite her reasoning mid-message. My favourite occasion was when she phoned to say that she wouldn't be coming in that day "because, er...because...oh, because I can't be arsed." She then promptly put thc phone down.

I can't tell you how many times staff played and replayed that message; snorts and cackles of laughter filled the reception area when each person came in that day and it was played once more. I thought Linda was marvellous and she could make me laugh without even trying. Whenever she did finally return, I loved to hear about her antics, as well as admiring her photos of the wonderful "panoromantic views". These scenes depicted an array of gentlemen friends with whom she'd become acquainted, set against a sun-drenched vista. It's little wonder she needed a couple of weeks to recover after she returned!

Having Brenda in charge of HR was unwise given that she perhaps didn't possess the requisite skill set. Nor did she fully appreciate the discretion essential for the undertaking.

Occasionally, there was accidental information seepage from staff, and Brenda would hear about something which she hadn't yet been told by the individual concerned. This was due to them not wanting her to know, undoubtedly because the individual didn't want it casually shared with others or would want to share the information in their own time. Accordingly, when Brenda discovered the information or just fragments, she'd morph into 'Mystic Brenda' to extract the full details she desired from the person concerned.

So, perhaps if she'd discovered a positive pregnancy test in the toilet, she'd wistfully stare at the individual to whom she thought it belonged, while mobilising and twirling one of her many lengthy chin hairs. Then, with a pensive and preoccupied look on her face, she'd claim that there was something "a bit different" about them and that she was sensing something new in their "auric field". Then she'd go on to say that she just couldn't get songs with the word "baby" in their lyrics out of her head, and these earworms had been plaguing her since she'd woken up that morning. She even sang a few lines from various hits. I'd never seen anything like it. Some people stared at her blankly, while the ones who knew how to manage her played along with the façade.

Brenda might well have always possessed metaphysical attributes and access to higher spiritual realms. However, these celestial gifts were only evident when she was seeking information.

Although my anxiety was often elevated, this was sometimes tempered by the regular laughs meted out by the office environment. I often giggled, but even now, I cannot decide whether it was the clients who were humorous or the staff's handling and interpretation of them that coloured and breathed life into the comical situations that were relentless. Some of the staff managed to crystallise a client's shortcomings or idiosyncrasies with a simple expression or gesture, and I was always impressed by such a skill as I could never distil so much into so little.

There were loads of interesting clients. There was 'Mexican-Wave-Dave', aptly named because he had stunted arms. Then there was 'Tower-Block-Tim' who was, as his name suggested, very tall. Tim came on his bicycle, which he secured outside of the office, and the reception staff kept an eye on it for him. I never saw the bicycle, although given his height, nothing short of a penny-farthing would keep him aloft. Then, there was the client with his tag fitted to his prosthetic leg. He would switch to his spare prosthetic leg and go out and commit further offences. Or there was the client who was linked to a massive bag of heroin, as she'd left her National Insurance card in the bag because she'd used it to cut the drug and draw up the lines. However, my all-time favourite would have to be Roy.

Roy was a fascinating character who possessed spectacular, and almost unrivalled delusions of grandeur. His cut-glass eloquence and smooth, deliberate delivery were made even more poignant by his impeccable manners and immaculate tweed attire. He looked and dressed like a quintessential English country gent from the nineteenth century, who'd just been fitted out at a hunting apparel outfitter, complete with a deerstalker hat.

Whenever we met, Roy took great pains to remind me of his regal lineage and links to the British and French aristocracy. Seemingly, 1981 was a busy year for Roy as he was made a lord, a marquis, an earl and a duke. He was also ordained by the Orthodox Church and was the reincarnation of Saint Francis of Assisi. Roy also received professorships from numerous prestigious universities. When we didn't meet in person, he'd write me letters on linen paper in fountain pen, which showcased his beautiful handwriting; his letters were like scrolls. Each of his letters reiterated his astonishing credentials in the first instance and then progressed onto the substance of the correspondence, which often paled into insignificance compared to his accolades and titles.

Sometimes, Roy would write to me about aspects of his criminal case. Then, other times, he'd tell me all about the problems he was having with the council, along with their tardiness when it came to fixing the damp patch on his bedroom wall and attending to the broken lifts and rubbish on the communal stairs. However, as I was not instructed on a housing matter, I could do little to assist with these difficulties. I advised him of this and suggested that I refer him to a colleague who dealt with housing issues.

Other times, he'd write informing me that as the council were fitting his new bathroom, coupled with his mouth ulcer, he would, therefore, be precluded from attending the Criminal Court the following week for his trial. Roy assured me that the judge would understand. I replied, explaining how I thought the court would take a dim view of his failure to attend, as his reasons were unlikely to be considered acceptable by the judge. Therefore, if he didn't want a warrant for his arrest to be issued, he'd best be there and on time.

One of Roy's concerns was that the press would hound him at court, and the paparazzi would sit in the public gallery and write terrible stories about him, given his regal ties and aristocratic links. I explained that this was unlikely to be the case and that he shouldn't concern himself with this but should instead focus on getting to court and seeing the pharmacist about his mouth ulcer.

Roy would write to officials and foreign dignitaries, and send them signed photographs of himself in regal robes trimmed with ermine fur. Then once again, he'd catalogue his titles, appointments and positions; I suppose this was in case they'd forgotten. Roy thought there'd be no harm in engaging in some cordial communication, and he even extended the hand of friendship to some, inviting them to apply for positions of employment on his team, as they might wish to join his courtiers and when not waiting on Roy, they could assist his French chefs in the Victorian kitchens of his palatial abode.

Roy preferred written correspondence as it would appear that 'The Authorities', i.e., those who spoke to him and furnished him with instructions, had told him to unplug his phone. Nonetheless, if I needed to contact him, Roy left it plugged in for one hour per day ("between 03:00 Hr – 04:00 Hr"). Sometimes, instructions from Roy were sporadic, but this was because he was awaiting his next set of instructions from 'The Authorities'. Roy usually relied on just one or two media of communication with his superiors. The university seemingly preferred FM radio waves; however, if they could not reach him through this method, they defaulted to rear car registration plates to convey messages. Certain combinations of digits and letters apparently held specific messages and instructions to him.

Having spent years awaiting his next set of instructions from 'The Authorities', Roy developed some insight for a while into his delusions.

He was devastated to discover that he wasn't all that he thought he was, and I felt incredibly sad for him. That's not to say I'm minimising his behaviours or their impact on others, but it must be shattering to discover none of the grandiosity you've attributed to yourself is true. I hope he never encountered any of those aristocratic photos when he was well, as they could have been challenging to come to terms with.

Some days, I felt emotionally depleted. It is typical for many autistic people to struggle with too much people contact. It can wipe us out. I've known autistic children to have meltdowns, and although I don't have meltdowns, I often felt the need to disconnect completely. This was usually because I was just overwhelmed. Still, I'd also become hyper-vigilant in anticipation of the inevitability of the next Brenda-based eruption, which I was always keen to circumvent if I possibly could.

One of the lawyers I worked with told me that the kind of cases the firm encountered were extraordinary and extreme, and I should remember that wherever I might work in the future. In her opinion, a small number of the cases were routine while the vast majority were unusual or had exceptional aspects, and I might never encounter cases or clients like them again, and she wasn't wrong. While my resilience grew and I became a little less unnerved by colleagues and cases alike, before long, nothing surprised me. I don't think I appreciated that working in some types of law provided such a unique insight into the human condition.

Hangovers, swearing, smoking lots of fags and eating copious amounts of fried food and sugar were all very much part of the daily rhythm of the place, but so was the law. I was very fortunate to have the opportunity to work with some super bright people, undertaking some incredible work on some extraordinary cases. Publicly funded lawyers aren't paid handsome salaries; they do it because the cases are often very interesting, and they are passionate about facilitating justice for those who need it but can't afford to pay.

Listening to some of them discuss matters was fascinating, although I remember on a few occasions, some discussions became quite arduous. I love semantics and nuances with the best of the pedants, but I sometimes remember thinking it was like listening to a bunch of bald blokes argue over a hairbrush.

I was often able to assist, albeit in a minor way, with some remarkable matters, although it must be said that I was just as fascinated by clients and their antics as much as the legal points in question. Some lawyers would complain about the firm's pay, conditions and 'Brendafication', and I'd ask them why they stayed. Some did leave, but there were some who'd been there a while and always said the same thing – because the nature and quality of work were second to none.

There were varying levels of technology and I.T. skills within the firm, and as someone who loved technology, computers and gadgets, I never understood how some people were either uncomfortable or bewildered by it. That said, I don't understand makeup or social nuances, so I've had to remind myself not to judge and to check my privilege.

One of the lawyers, who disliked and was unprepared for technology, was given a smartphone. That wasn't unusual for an office environment, but her response was. She could be found trailing around the building, holding it up to the window, trying to work out which end to speak into and looking at it bemused and alarmed. Sometimes, she just stood in the middle of the office with it in her hand, staring at it. Smartphones were commonplace in all work environments at this time, so it was remarkable that they generated such bewilderment. This device would get left in all sorts of places, and she always looked crestfallen when it was returned to her. I'll never know how it found its way into the kitchen cupboards and office toilet cabinet.

When it rang, she ignored it, and it was full of unread text messages. If it made "a squeak", as she called it, she'd try and hand it to someone to resolve. If you took it off her, you'd accepted the invitation, and you had to then take her through the arduous processes once more, namely, how to answer it, how to open a text, how to make a call, etc., and this could wipe out a considerable period of time. It didn't matter how often she was taken through it; it didn't sink in.

I didn't think people like that existed in this day and age, although I should have known how technologically inept she was when I found her waiting at the fax machine for something to come out. She thought it was the printer. She was there for ages. Fortunately, she had her new smartphone to stare at. It wasn't until one of the secretaries, a true mouth-breather who didn't like to rush anything, got tired of waiting for her fax that the queue dispersed.

Working there was sometimes like being in a Hall of Mirrors, to utilise a circus or fairground analogy once again. Sometimes, things didn't seem real because so much was extreme and distorted. It didn't matter where I worked in the building and with whom; somebody was always sporting an orange face, large gold sovereign rings and celebrating the fact that they were not pregnant that month.

I recall one morning when I'd had a particularly large dose of 'Regal Roy', and I'd had to see another delusional criminal client named Adrian. Ordinarily, I was sheltered from clients visiting me ad lib, as they had to either have an appointment or negotiate with reception before they could access lawyers. Even if you said you were busy, the reception staff would put the clients in an interview room as they wanted them out of reception and out of their way. However, on this occasion, I'd just been seeing Roy out and was nabbed by Adrian, who was on his way in, so I had no choice.

From day one, Adrian developed an immediate love and disdain for me in equal measure. Sometimes, he'd be my number one fan; other times, he'd tell me I was a diabolical human being. Adrian could nearly always be found in a multicoloured cheesecloth top, a sequined waistcoat, wooden beads around his neck and no shoes or socks. He was also seldom seen without a small bongo drum tucked under his left arm. I am sure he could pass for Jesus in an amateur production with his long dark hair, wispy beard and prophetic soliloquies.

The dichotomy between Adrian's loving and loathing of me, which could switch at any moment, was unfathomable. On this particular occasion, he was convinced that I worked for both MI5 *and* MI6 simultaneously. My assurances to the contrary did nothing to assuage his fixed beliefs, and he remained convinced that I was associated with "men in dark suits" and "covert military personnel", the very same individuals, incidentally, who just the other day had been operating on his brain. Adrian didn't want or need to see me; he was "just passing", which was even worse as I didn't know why I was standing there having my non-existent security service credentials questioned. Just then, and for no apparent reason, he hugged me, offered me a £0.50 voucher for the fried chicken shop and left.

As Adrian left, he was nearly run over by the old lady who lived nearby and drove a mobility scooter. She was rapid – lead foot to the floor. She was so fast that the force of driving into the wind almost left her devoid of any wrinkles. She didn't look left or right; she just powered straight on, and anyone with any sense got out of her way as soon as they saw her coming. I think she must have had that machine customised.

I had never anticipated that back-to-back delusions and raging paranoia would be a normal part of my day-to-day work, but it was. That said, I found these situations less stressful and intimidating than when Brenda was volcanic and spewing molten affronts whenever she received any kind of vaguely bad news.

This was because although Adrian and Roy's mindboggling delusions left me poleaxed for the most part, along with the fact that they were frenetic and unpredictable, which is the absolute antithesis of a conducive environment for me, there was no angry swearing or hostility. I think that's what I found so difficult to tolerate, be it directed towards myself or colleagues. Abuse of power is difficult to call out at the best of times and has always left me feeling neuralgic; however, when one has absolutely no means of redress other than leaving, the feeling of being defenceless and without recourse is hollowing.

Towards the end of my time "working in crime", I received a letter from Roy. It would appear that he'd recently been advised by 'The Authorities' (via rear car number plates) that it had transpired that he had further ancient royal ancestry, and so he now assumed the title of emperor. I imagine he wasted no time in getting his camera dusted off. I wondered what attire he'd wear for the photo shoot.

Denise would host a regular criminal departmental meeting, and all criminal lawyers were expected to attend. I think it's fair to say that there was a somewhat 'male locker room' banter, and it must be said the women were the worst. Denise got through forty minutes' worth of information in twenty minutes flat. This was mainly due to how quickly she spoke and rattled everything off. Denise was also a dab hand at multitasking and was most definitely polytropic. While speaking at speed, she still managed to text the clients due in court that morning to ensure they were awake, so she didn't need to have a battle about who was going to the police station later when they were picked up on a warrant.

Having wagged her finger and insisted that people not be rude to one another, Denise would then inform everyone how one of the "barking clients" had been let out of the "nuthouse" and had come through via the Police Station Rota the previous night. As there were no takers in the first instance, she'd say, "Right, dickhead, you do it!" while pointing at whomever had recently got on her nerves or not brought her chicken in a basket back when they'd been for one themselves. It didn't matter when the meeting took place; a similar theme ran through each one.

On another occasion, there was a disagreement about who would attend the "cop shop" to see a client whose head lice were said to have been seen "pole vaulting" from some distance. The "lice file" was hurled around the room like an incendiary device, and nobody was prepared to take it of their own volition.

The "dickhead" who was told to go was a lawyer who was outraged and emphatically against the notion. She stroked her long silky hair and looked around the room, beseeching someone more follically suited to take up the quest. Just then, she had an epiphany as the morning sun bounced off the shiny head of a bald bloke opposite her and she decided that she'd found her target audience. She petitioned hard for him to go, and a trade-off for some unfavourable police station rota slot sealed the deal.

The meetings kicked off early and although most managed to get there by the skin of their teeth, scrambling to their seats, that's all that could be said. During the meeting, some would yawn while eating their breakfast and continued to dress in ties and cufflinks they had not quite managed to get on before leaving home. I even recall one of the lawyers trimming her fringe (with no mirror) during discussions and another painting her nails.

Although I was "working in crime", and I usually had my head in a criminal file or could be found taking a statement off a client, I wasn't immune from Brenda because she was omnipotent.

Brenda's 'car people' increased even more during the school holidays because children, as did one of their boyfriends, came in too. There were also times when younger children were brought in and were underwhelmed at having to be there. Now, it wasn't just the exhaust; one could hear bickering and arguing halfway up the street as there were loads of them and having no volume control was a family trait.

It was mayhem from the moment they crashed through the door first thing on a morning. One child had a long face following a row with the boyfriend; the boyfriend was unsure how to respond to a tirade of verbal abuse, and the younger children were not happy about being there at all. School holidays were longer than I recalled, and bored children would mooch around the office, text friends and play on the internet while the rhythm of the office never missed a beat. One child even took a computer to bits and put it all back together, with enough components left to make a small radio.

I recall one occasion when Brenda's fuse was somewhat shorter than normal due to school holidays, and it was quite frightening. She'd stormed out of her office walking like a woman on a mission, having discovered for the umpteenth time that month that no funding had been applied for on a file and that the firm wouldn't be paid for the not inconsiderable work undertaken so far. I can understand why she was annoyed; however, she couldn't contain or regulate her emotions long enough to tackle the person in question. Instead, she erupted in the middle of the office, emitting such anger that her face migrated through every shade of purple on a paint swatch colour chart.

Luckily for that particular lawyer, they were out of the office as her rage ricocheted around the building. So, as was all too common, everybody else was berated and sworn at despite it having absolutely nothing to do with them. In situations like that, there was a good chance that Brenda might have forgotten, so if you were the offending staff member, you'd have to hope that something more important came up, which could result in her shifting her wrath elsewhere.

As Brenda stormed out and as the rest of the room remained head downward pointing, one of the lawyers walked in, all flustered and preoccupied, and it wasn't anything to do with the unfunded file. She composed herself and asked everyone, as casually as she could, if they'd "seen the work experience boy"?

Nobody had, and all were just relieved that Brenda and her hostility had left, at least for now. It would appear that we had a schoolboy undertaking some work experience with us. The previous day, the lawyer had taken him to court so that he could watch the law in action. However, she'd woken up in the night sweating and frantic. "Jesus Christ! I've left the work experience boy in Court Two!" It would appear that she'd left him in there to attend another courtroom to collect something, had then become distracted, forgotten about him altogether and then gone home. It was only the next day, in the early morning hours when she suddenly sat bolt upright in bed, that she remembered him. Anyhow, nobody appeared remotely concerned.

I suggested that I call the courts to see if anybody had handed him in or if they could at least provide any further details. I asked her his name, but she couldn't remember it and her attempts to describe him could have been of any child.

We never did find out what happened to him because he never returned. Situations such as this proved to be a welcome distraction when Brenda was about to implode.

We'd frequently have work experience kids coming in to spend time in a law firm as some thought they wanted to study the law. I'm not sure if we did more harm than good, really. Nonetheless, they were given tasks. Some took them incredibly seriously, and others were there under duress. I remember one child being super enthusiastic when being asked to tidy up the files on the shelves, and it made a refreshing change not to have a child grunting from behind a curtain of hair.

What should have been a quick job took him all day. Nobody checked on what he was doing. When I went into the room, the shelves were spotless. No random files were pushed into tiny gaps, in the wrong places or upside down. I was impressed. I couldn't have done a better job of it myself.

However, I soon realised that it was too good to be true. It would appear that the child hadn't been provided with adequate instructions, which was no great surprise. Every file had been put in alphabetical order based on the client's forename, not the surname. So, John Smith was under J, which was problematic enough, but when you have names like Xavier under Z and Philip Jones under F, it took quite a while to find some files.

Criminal defence work was very interesting, a real eye-opener, and the clients were usually good to work with. I enjoyed working with the lawyers, and they knew after working with me for some months that they could rely upon me to get the job done, just as long as they took responsibility for what they needed to do in terms of providing clarity and specific details.

I enjoyed building the files for court, looking at the evidence presented by the CPS, and then carefully going through it. However, as I approached the end of my time in that seat, I knew it wasn't an area I wanted to pursue.

I became disenchanted and, to some extent, exasperated at the idea that some people offended so frequently they were regulars. There was a real 'revolving door' nature to some clients' offending, and I struggled with that. Of course, lots of criminal defence work relies upon a relatively small number of returning clientele, but it wasn't for me long-term as I didn't really see any kind of rehabilitation, and that frustrated me.

Chapter 6
Mental Health

Having finished "working in crime", Mental Health was my second seat. I'd be both in and out of the office during this time. Some clients did come to the office, but most were in the hospital wards in psychiatric units with varying levels of freedom.

Clients I encountered generally had a diagnosis of psychosis, bipolar disorder or schizophrenia and experienced many of the following: paranoia, delusions, thought transmission, thought intrusion and thought insertion, along with auditory, olfactory, visual and sensory hallucinations. Some could smell death, some thought they were being touched, some believed they were having thoughts inserted into their head, some heard voices saying derogatory things about them, and some even thought they were dead. These dreadful experiences must have been absolutely petrifying.

Floridly psychotic patients can experience disturbing and terrifying persecutory feelings and delusional thinking, so trying to take instructions from them could be exceptionally difficult. Many of the clients during my training made a real impact on me, but the clients with mental health conditions fascinated me above all, and I think my desire to help them, along with my feelings of helplessness, was overwhelming.

Some clients accepted that they were being detained on a ward under the Mental Health Act to be assessed by a specially trained team, but some sought to restore their liberty. When a patient is detained, checks and balances are in place to ensure that there isn't an abuse of state power. Therefore, a patient has the right to have their case heard at a Mental Health Tribunal. This is where an independent and knowledgeable panel will consider their case and see if they think the detention is justified. This will be based upon the evidence of medical staff and can be challenged by a lawyer familiar with Mental Health Tribunals. These hearings take place at the hospital in a quiet room.

I remember observing my first Mental Health Tribunal and thinking how daunting it must be for the client. Although the hearings were as informal as possible and not like a courtroom, they had a formality. Clients were legally represented; nonetheless, they must have felt completely overwhelmed by the process, especially as some would have been paranoid or suffering from persecutory ideations. Therefore, the idea of having a group of people sitting and talking about them must have been very disempowering, not to mention daunting.

A very formidable-looking lady chaired the first tribunal I attended. She was young in the face, but her sugar-spun hair and eyebrows drawn on with what looked like a black felt-tip pen made her look much older, and her fingers were stubby and chunky. She had a fake smile, lipstick on her teeth, and she'd have got on my nerves if I'd have been a patient before her at a tribunal. The chair was a giant of a woman and wore a pristine pinstriped suit which started off as pinstripe at her feet, but the further up her leg you looked, the stripes turned into a zebra crossing.

The hearings were as friendly as possible, and while clients were helped and supported, I couldn't help thinking how they were often futile. So many of the clients were so unwell they had little to no chance of being released, and I think that was the right decision for the most part.

One of the most poignant and enduring memories I have of mental health clients is how defenceless they were. This was partly due to how debilitating the conditions could be, but also by public perception and how certain systems were stacked against them, resulting in their being disempowered before they'd even started.

A client once asked something very meaningful during one of our meetings. "Why is it that everything a doctor says is evidence while everything I say is a delusion?"

It really made me think, and I began to appreciate what a disadvantage mental health clients, in general, were at. I understand why, but I do think what they have to say isn't always given validity by professionals.

The first client I came across was Stanley. The whole office was aware of Stanley. He never came in because he lived in a locked ward, but he often telephoned. When I came in on a morning, I would listen to one of the girls go through the previous evening's answerphone messages. We only knew that the maximum number of messages the machine could hold was fifteen because Stanley would consume the first fifteen slots, and then nobody else could leave a message after that, not even Stanley. We knew it was Stanley on the answerphone because although he seldom left his name or a message, he left his 'signature' swear words, a big sigh, a protracted huff and puff and then the final slamming down of the receiver.

Having done this fifteen times, he could not (indeed nor could anybody else) leave any more messages until the office reopened the next day and the machine was cleared and reset. Despite being told that the mental health lawyers did not work in reception (let alone work on reception around the clock), he'd call the office at all hours, wanting to speak to one of them. So, when he called at three o'clock in the morning, unsurprisingly, he just got the answerphone. Therefore, dealing with Stanley's fifteen overnight messages was part of the daily morning reception routine.

When I finally met Stanley, I learned about his fixation with a famous 1970s actress and sex symbol. According to Stanley, the two of them went way back. Stanley was convinced that he'd fathered twins with her, as well as siring at least twelve other children with a selection of hospital ward staff. This upset him because he didn't know how it'd happened.

During my first meeting with him, *apropos* of nothing, Stanley said he'd won two million pounds at the bingo. With his winnings, he claimed to have bought a famous football club, and should I ever wish to marry at the ground, I'd be most welcome to, he told me.

Before being admitted to the hospital, Stanley had thought he'd come into a large amount of money and had hired a stretch limo, complete with a bar, for all his friends on the estate to drive around in, eating fried chicken and burgers. Goodness knows what the staff at the drive-through must have thought when they pulled up. Stanley hadn't won a large amount of money; he'd paid for the food and excursion with his state benefits, but he thought he'd had a serious win, such were his delusions.

Stanley typified how vulnerable mental health conditions made people and what some medications did to the human body. I'm a great believer in advancing treatments and using whatever medication is necessary to treat the condition. However, some of the psychotropic medications can have a devastating impact on the body. Stanley had a dangerously high BMI and it would seem that the medications had significantly contributed to his having the physique of a gestating rhino. I think that a mental health condition, coupled with the side effects of some treatments, is the worst medical condition a person can have because the consequences of the treatment can create a whole new set of serious health problems, such as diabetes. What's more, the mental health condition is often lifelong and allows little to no respite.

Luke was another client who interested me because, evidently, he'd led a 'normal' life up to being admitted to hospital with bipolar disorder in his forties. His mania was off the chart when he was initially seen by me and whichever lawyer I'd been assigned to that day.

Luke had tremendous delusions of grandeur and thought he was one of the greatest boxers of all time. We saw Luke on a locked ward, and while instructions were sought, Luke proceeded to flit and dance around the room and encircled us, to the extent that he was looping the room while launching punches towards an imaginary opponent and talking about his next fight in Las Vegas and how this one was going to surpass all others. Luke must have been exhausted because we were with him for some time.

Trying to read a lengthy technical consultant's report with a client can be difficult in a conducive environment; however, trying to do so while the client is punching the air, dancing around the room, ducking imaginary blows and commentating on his own boxing performance has to be seen to be believed.

Fortunately, the living area was a large room with a lot of space for

Luke to shadowbox. Nevertheless, if I thought that taking instructions from the sausage roll brigade, complete with baby and dog on a string, in a tiny room back at the office was challenging, then this was unquestionably the next level up.

Not only a world-class boxer with a pending multimillion-dollar title challenge in Las Vegas, Luke claimed to have mended the ozone layer with a simple swipe of his hand over the heavens, such were his Messianic attributes. Having repaired the ozone, Luke developed a cancer cure after lunch the following week. It didn't take long, and he'd nailed it before dinner time.

It would appear that Luke also spent much of his time on Jupiter, where he had neighbourly disputes with the Dalai Lama. Luke believed that when he was not a famous boxer, he was Jesus Christ and verified this by showing us the acne scars on his forehead. He explained that the indentations were where his crown of thorns had been placed.

I learned an important lesson on the mental health wards: to ask for evidence of these fantastic claims. To dismiss them outright would have been wrong because what a client says is important and forms part of their instructions; however, accepting them without challenge is colluding with the delusions, which certainly wouldn't help them.

In this day and age, people are so afraid of being insensitive or inappropriate that the temptation is to agree and patronise, but that's counterproductive. It was clear that Luke was going to struggle to be released from state care and during the tribunal, he continued with his sparring, punching and boxing critique despite being told to stop.

During his tribunal, Luke's phone went off and he answered it. Luke then chatted with the caller and proceeded to ask for fish and chips to be brought in. The panel members just sat and waited for him to finish his call, but he wasn't in a rush. Once he'd finished his chat, I remember him trying to negotiate with the Tribunal Chair when he'd devised a compromise to his being on a locked ward, and this entailed his using the hospital as his "base", with a view to being released, going about his boxing career and "checking in and out" as and when, so as to mollify the overanxious staff.

Luke's request was declined, and he wasn't successful on that occasion. He took the news remarkably well, as I recall, and then proceeded to show us twenty-seven photos he had taken of the bathroom, all from different angles. He went through all of the pictures with us and explained which of his relatives they were, one by one. We saw his mum, his dad and his brother. When we'd reached the twenty-seventh picture, he was asked who it was. Surprised and a little perturbed, he said, "That's the toilet, dickhead."

Sometimes, clients were remarkably comical; however, listening to their delusions was also incredibly sad, and it bothered me enormously.

I encountered Adrian again sometime later. His persecutory delusions had escalated, and his mental health had deteriorated even further. There were no offers of hugs or £0.50 vouchers for the fried chicken shop. I discovered that he believed that he'd had a stroke due to poisons being placed in the cheese he had bought from the supermarket. Mental health staff took Adrian to the ward where stroke victims were recovering to show him what a stroke does to a person and their body, but he still thought he'd had a stroke despite being shown how incapacitating a stroke was.

Adrian then went on to accuse another supermarket of putting toxins in their milk, which resulted in him having a brain tumour. Adrian believed that he was being sprayed with poisons by the security services because he'd told the world that they'd murdered members of the royal family, and now they were seeking retribution by making him look paranoid when, in reality, he was the only one who could see what was going on.

Life for Adrian must have been petrifying because he genuinely believed he was being poisoned and harassed. Adrian spent much of his time contacting government agencies demanding action be taken against MI5. Although his beliefs were genuine, there was no evidence to suggest any validity in his food poisoning claims. He and others like him must have made the people he spoke with wonder what was happening.

I remember one client who believed that he'd had a sex change imposed upon him and that because he was raped every night, he'd become pregnant. He believed that staff members were poisoning him on the ward, and they had also secretly operated on his body against his will. His nihilistic delusions (he believed he was dead) were overwhelming and permeated everything he said. Just when I thought I couldn't be any more shocked, I was quite stunned when we completed his forms together in order for the public purse to fund the costs of his having a lawyer to represent him on this mental health matter.

Now, this was a client who was in a locked ward and who had a string of unsuccessful Mental Health Tribunals behind him. As I reached the section which necessitated questions about ethnicity and disability monitoring, I asked him if he was disabled or if he thought he had a disability. He looked at me aghast, and I think he was almost offended.

In fact, he, like many of the mental health clients I encountered, answered with an emphatic and firm 'no' to this question. It really made me think, because what's a disability to one person clearly isn't to another and as it can be self-defining, two people with the same condition could provide a very different response.

I, on the other hand, am not on a locked ward and do believe that the conditions I have mean that I have a disability, not just because I fulfil the criteria set by legislation, but because I need adjustments to be made for me in many respects to make my life either a bit easier or some things at all possible.

Sadly, I think there's still a great deal of stigma associated with mental illness, which I think may prohibit some people from either seeking help or, for that matter, considering themselves as having a disability at all; but I also think that some people may not know what legally constitutes a disability.

Some people think they need to be unable to walk to qualify as disabled because, after all, the disability symbol found on toilets and in Blue Badge parking areas is a person in a wheelchair, and if that alone was what entitled somebody to declare a disability, then the number of disabled people in the UK would be artificially low.

However, more importantly, in my opinion, if you needed to be a wheelchair user to be considered disabled, the legal protections such as in the workplace and education, to name but a few areas, would not help and support those who needed help while allowing employers and service providers to evade their duties and responsibilities, and for me, that's not an option.

Legal protections are in place to help and assist; refuse them if you wish, but I just want people to make informed decisions.

Poor mental health knows no class or wealth barriers. It can affect a duke or a dustman and can strike at any time in one's life. I remember two very different clients at tribunals around the same time; one was a middle-class affluent lady named Sophia, and the other was a working-class man named Doug who was on benefits. They couldn't have been more different – socially, economically or educationally.

Doug believed he'd made not billions, not trillions, but zillions of pounds on online auction sites. He believed he'd bought expensive cars for £1 and sold them for £100,000. According to Doug, he'd purchased many luxury items for pennies and then sold each item for an eye-watering profit. When talking to us, Doug explained how he was flabbergasted as to why everybody wasn't doing the same because it was the easiest money he'd ever made. Believing he'd made so much money, Doug cancelled all of his benefits because he no longer required financial assistance. Following this grand gesture, Doug found himself in increasingly compromising situations, resulting in his being detained under the Mental Health Act.

Doug's tribunal went ahead. He wasn't 'bouncing off the walls' or boxing around the room as some did, and he came across well. He articulated himself intelligently and engaged well with the panel. He answered all of the questions put to him, and, for a while at least, I thought we were in with a really good chance of the tribunal finding in our favour, which would mean that Doug would no longer be detained and deprived of his liberty. However, right at the end, when one of the panel members asked about his newfound wealth and business ventures, it deteriorated fast. I could see our chances of winning and all our hard work unravelling and disintegrating. It was like watching a car crash; you could not do anything to prevent it from happening, and it was painful to watch, but it was going to happen, come what may, and there was nothing anybody could do. Doug explained how there were a lot of expensive things like houses, watches or countries that were only £1 on the online auction sites that you could buy and then sell for a million or a billion pounds. Over one weekend, he'd made zillions, "piece of piss", evidently. I knew from the moment the word "zillion" was uttered that that was it for Doug, and his quest for freedom would be on hold, at least for a while, which is just what happened.

Sophia also had bipolar disorder and had led a 'normal' life, with a regular suburban existence, a husband and a few children. This was right up to being picked up by the police, having been found walking into oncoming traffic on a motorway, wearing just an elf costume. When we saw her, she was in the grip of a fully-fledged manic episode. She exhibited several classic features of the condition, including pressured speech, flight of ideas, grandiosity, irritability, shouting and ranting. However, this was compounded by the fact that she was a phenomenally high-maintenance diva. Sophia flipped from hysterical laughter to weeping and wailing like a banshee within the space of two minutes, and it wasn't easy to anticipate her next mood. One hour with her felt like five, and I was exhausted by her level of output because she was emotionally draining.

Taking any kind of instructions from Sophia was a labour-intensive task. The first time I met her, she consistently needed peeling off the ceiling and trying to follow not just the content but the speed of her monologues and eulogies was taxing. Sophia was not like the other mental health clients who often forgot to wash or to change their clothes and reeked of stale cigarettes. She spoke as though she was blue-blooded, and our first meeting with her opened in style.

The door was flung open, and a Lilliputian stick insect flounced into the room. She strutted in like a catwalk model, crossing her legs over one another as she glided along. Her face was solemn, and her makeup was exquisitely applied, making her look very Parisian while oozing wall-to-wall attitude and pizzazz. She was kitted out in state-of-the-art haute couture and carried a microscopic handbag and a stylish walking cane, which, incidentally, Roy would have loved.

Throughout our time together, Sophia had tantrums at ten-minute intervals and changed her clothes countless times. It wouldn't take much to trigger a meltdown, and off she'd flounce to her nearby room, only to return a couple of minutes later wearing an entirely new wardrobe, top to toe, and often exhibiting (albeit for a limited time) quite a different demeanour.

Having entered the room in style, Sophia would ritualistically load and unload the contents of her minuscule handbag. She told us that she was above answering questions, talked over us every time one of us said anything, regularly admired herself in a personalised compact mirror and applied perfume every six to eight minutes.

When Sophia entered the tribunal room, she immediately became heartbroken and sobbed uncontrollably because everybody wore suits and nobody was wearing wigs or gowns. She wanted a proper court with proper people who were suitably attired, and money was no object. Moreover, she made sure they all knew that she looked fabulous and expected them to look marvellous, too.

The entire process had been explained to her on more than one occasion. However, she did not afford the process much gravitas from thereon, as people weren't dressed appropriately, in her opinion. During the hearing, she'd regularly apply lashings of perfume, top up her lipstick, and even got out a glossy magazine at one point, crossed her legs and flicked through the pages.

Before long, she'd had a row with the chair as she did not like being told *she* couldn't cross-examine the panel. The dispute was followed by her informing the chair that she intended to sue her as she didn't know how important she was.

Things then went from bad to worse when we once again put the questions to Sophia we'd asked before the hearing to 'tease out' information/answers to help her case. While giving evidence, she furiously snapped that she'd told us all of this before and that we needed to get our memories checked out. Moreover, we should make some notes in future and listen more attentively. Once again, the fury turned to tears, followed by her handing me a wad of cash and a demand to pay her credit card bill.

This intelligent, cultured and educated woman had turned into something quite unrecognisable and, needless to say, was unsuccessful at her tribunal, which was yet another catalyst for a further eruption.

I saw her sometime later, and I cannot tell you what a difference I saw in her. She'd responded well to medication and was a totally different person.

I've noticed two interesting things about mental illness, which Doug and Sophia typified. Firstly, while some people discriminate against those with a mental health condition, mental health conditions don't themselves discriminate. They can and indeed do strike anybody at any time, regardless of class or demographic. Secondly, mental illness can bring some very unlikely people together.

Doug and Sophia got on remarkably well. They were in the same unit and spent much time together. They were from very different backgrounds, and I suspect that their paths would never ordinarily have crossed; however, the mental illness they shared had broken down barriers, especially class and the stigma of mental health.

Whenever I was on a mental health ward, more time was spent trying to locate the clients than anything else. The vast majority were prolific smokers, and the knack was working out where they'd gone to smoke, which could be anywhere, although many had their favourite locations within the confines of the locked areas. However, when I finally located them, no matter how long I spent with them, I never quite mastered the art of taking their instructions.

This wasn't because they'd walk off mid-sentence or I couldn't always find them; it was because their thinking was so disordered, and no matter how much I tried to introduce order and structure into my questioning, it was largely to no avail. Some of them were as nebulous as Brenda, albeit for very different reasons.

A one-hour appointment might provide no more than a smattering of lucid and cogent instructions for me to work with. I encountered this not only when I worked in mental health but also in other areas with clients suffering from mental health conditions.

I really struggled with clients' thought processes, which were seldom linear or fathomable, and this was so important for me in terms of how I think and process information because I battle at the best of times with focus. So when somebody has a chaotic thought pattern, it's like trying to drive a car on ice with the handbrake on.

I decided the best method for me was either to speak to them in the smoking area, as they loved being there and would be reasonably still for at least five minutes, or to try to get the most hectic clients to give me 'the headlines' in the first instance; that way I was most likely to quickly get to the heart of the matter and take it from there.

Another thing I noticed about working in mental health was that most clients regularly talked about how everybody else around them was "far more mental" than they could ever dream of being. They'd even look in pity at some of the other patients on the ward because seemingly, they were more mental.

They'd then go into detail and tell you just *how* mental the others on the ward were and how *they* were nowhere near as mental as the rest; there appeared to almost be a 'mentalness hierarchy'. The level of mentalness some clients did or didn't share became quite competitive at times, and I was privy to full-scale stand-up rows about who was the least mental because this ensured a higher status in their opinions.

I recall meeting my first client with body dysmorphic disorder, which I didn't know much about. This is when somebody is obsessively preoccupied with an aspect of their body, and it causes them considerable distress. Having visited this gentleman to take instructions, he wouldn't engage with us at all except to tell us that he was called Howard, his favourite subject at school was sex education, and he also expanded a little with regards to how much he hated his hand, which was his particular fixation. I assume that his hand had previously looked perfectly normal. However, we couldn't tell as it was covered in bandages following his attempts to remove it with an axe, because he believed that an evil entity possessed it.

Although we had few instructions, the tribunal went ahead. Howard entered the tribunal room, and all the normal procedural aspects took place. For some reason, Howard had come into the room without wearing shoes or socks. During the hearing, I looked down at his feet and wondered why he'd developed such a fixation with his hand when his feet were far more peculiar. When I think about it, it was a bit like a football game on television. Before the game, the camera slowly sweeps along the line-up of players and as the camera moves along, the commentator will say things like, "Here's this person and that person, they've had a good season, etc." Then the camera shoots vertically upwards to capture an incredibly tall player, and then it drops back down again, and the commentator continues to introduce the rest of the team and comment upon their performance during the season. Well, this client's toes were like a football team line-up, but made of toes, not people. The first two were of normal size, but the middle one was the length of a matchbox (and we're talking fat Kim's matches). Then, the rest of the toes were normal length again. I think podiatry journals world-wide would surely want to do a feature on Howard's enormous toe. It was incredible.

The more time I spent in tribunals, the more questions I had. I accepted that the clients had serious mental health conditions and were a potential risk; however, everything they said or did was 'medicalised', and there appeared to be minimal scope for the usual range of human manifestations and behaviours to exist without everything being examined and questioned.

If an individual was 'chatty', they might be labelled 'disinhibited' by staff. If a patient was 'untidy', they could be called 'dysfunctional'. If they wanted a bit of 'peace and quiet', they were 'disengaged' and so on. Everything patients did was so highly scrutinised. Admittedly, your average person isn't on a locked ward, but there are so many different manifestations of humans. I did think that sometimes these poor sods couldn't do right for doing wrong.

Patients spent their lives under the microscope while detained under the Mental Health Act in hospital. When you read the medical notes and see the level to which they're observed, it's little wonder some were paranoid.

Furthermore, the clinicians who have so much power and influence over people's liberty may be scientifically qualified to comment on their condition(s); however, a lot of the psychiatrists whom I've come across seem to possess extremely limited interpersonal and social skills. Therefore, in my opinion, they were not always best suited to assess the above. How can such individuals be qualified to assess the character and prognosis of an individual when they are so socially inept themselves?

This was not the organisation to work at when you're somebody who needs certainty and consistency. That said, a lot of the unanticipated things were comical. At times, the hilarity alone went some way to assuaging my all too often crippling anxiety, which was extremely loyal and never left my side.

I never knew what I was returning to in the office when I'd been out all day on the wards. If Brenda wasn't causing havoc, it wasn't uncommon for the cleaner to be on the warpath. She left some extremely sweary notes, and with good reason, to be fair, as staff seldom returned their dirty plates, bowls and cups to the kitchen.

There were invariably many half-consumed mugs of tea dispersed around the building, and some, which hadn't been located, were eventually found later, riddled with mould. Sometimes, they were lined up on a windowsill; other times, they were under desks and up on shelves. Brenda went through a phase of putting every dirty mug she found straight into the office bin, so staff soon bought some more and mended their ways by throwing the contents out of the window and then taking the crockery downstairs. If staff worked on one of the upper levels, it wasn't unheard of for an unsuspecting member of the public to get covered in old tea, but as it could have come from any number of windows from any number of offices, nothing was ever said.

When Brenda was in a good mood, she could be positively exuberant. Her buoyancy was usually short-lived, and she regularly took it too far; nonetheless, her antics sometimes made me chuckle, although not everybody laughed, and some just tutted and rolled their eyes because they'd seen it all before.

On one occasion, when I was in the office for the day, I was passing through reception, and the phones were busy, so I sat down and took a few calls. Within less than a minute of sitting at the desk, there was a loud bang on the window, which faced a road, shops, offices, pedestrians and traffic. As I spoke to the client on the phone and took the message, I looked up to see what on earth had hit the window, as I thought somebody had hurled a rock or something similar. It wasn't a missile; it was Brenda, looking in at the window and roaring with laughter. She'd lifted up her top, and all I could see was boobs and belly meat smeared across the window, frame to frame. As soon as her top went up, it went down again; she stuck two fingers up at me and hollered, "See you next week, big tits!" and trundled off, nursing her prolapsed womb. I always hoped that the womb would remain in situ for at least as long as I was working there, as the prospect of scooping it up off some carpet or trying to locate fragments of it made me shudder.

When Brenda left at the end of the day, occasionally a speaker announcement went out. Sometimes, there were rounds of applause and sighs of relief, especially if she'd been particularly egregious that day. The convention always reminded me of the close of trading at a stock exchange when they clap and you could tell by some of the comments that some staff knew how those East Germans felt when the wall fell in 1989.

I felt a bit sad as I approached the end of my time in mental health. I knew that would mean no longer receiving phone calls from princesses, kings, rock stars, pianists, artists, KGB agents and senior clergy members (including the Pope), and I knew I'd miss it. When clients rang, they often included their assumed persona in the conversation, so they'd ask for a call back before lunch as they had a meeting with the cardinals later. Alternatively, they'd ask for a visit but not on Tuesday because they'd be on stage or touring.

I also knew I'd miss the antics of some of the reception staff too, especially when they had taken a call for me from a mental health client. Sometimes, they'd email me; other times, they'd come into whichever room I was in, and I'd have to guess who had phoned by their rendition of whatever song the client's assumed character was famous for. On occasion, they'd even come up with backing singers or dancers. I had performances from different decades and they were often joined by their own dance company of secretaries. When I knew the artist, I'd know the client unless there were two, which wasn't unheard of.

There was an array of Broadway stars as well, along with singers from the Las Vegas Strip. However, not everybody was a celebrity. Some were just very important. We had one woman who believed she was a cardinal in her own church. She didn't do things by half; she had a dog collar, wore a great big cross around her neck and carried a mitre under her arm for when she received guests.

Now that I think about it, perhaps she wasn't mentally ill. Perhaps she'd just got sick of waiting for religious establishments to catch up and treat women equally, and knowing that the church wasn't particularly egalitarian, she'd set up her own – and who could blame her?

Chapter 7
Prison

Working with clients who have been convicted of serious criminal offences was very much part of my third seat, as I had the opportunity to work on the files of some of society's most prolific and dangerous offenders. Some of these people had grown up and matured in prison because they'd been there for so long and from such a young age. Some finished their formal education in prison, while others were just starting it.

Undertaking work with clients in prison also enabled me to see the daily workings and mechanics of the Parole Board, Probation Service, prisons and courts, and it was an absolute eye-opener. When we see an offender sentenced or up for parole on television, we aren't usually shown the whole 'machine' that operates around them; we just see the headline or outcome, but when I saw it all in action, at all different stages, so many parts of my classroom learning around Public Law clicked into place and became relevant.

Clients in prison, particularly those serving long sentences, often took a genuine interest in the legalities and particulars of their cases and took the time to inform themselves of their rights. Some read avidly about the law. Many understood the burdens of proof, thresholds to be overcome and tests that needed to be met.

Prison Law clients were sometimes subjected to treatment, which gave rise to our making an application for a Judicial Review. This is where a judge is asked to review the lawfulness of a decision or action taken by a public body, for example, a prison, the Parole Board or Probation Service. There were many such bodies involved with the care, treatment and progression of prisoners and sometimes, their decision-making and processes fell short of what one might expect. You may be surprised how frequently our public bodies fall short of being lawful; I know I was.

Clients were delighted when there were legal grounds in their case for a Judicial Review because it brought with it kudos and status for some. They knew Judicial Reviews weren't undertaken easily, and there was a long and sometimes arduous process involved in taking one right up to the court door and even then, the judge might disagree. Many would proudly tell other inmates that their case was being put before a judge because they knew it wasn't an everyday occurrence.

Even though we'd advise the client that the judge could only look at how a decision was made and couldn't change the decision themselves, it didn't seem to matter because they were being listened to. Their grudge or grievance was being taken seriously by someone in the know.

Some clients would ring up specifically requesting a 'JR', as it was colloquially known, and were disappointed when they learned that there were no grounds for one in their case. They loved to take on 'The Establishment' and win and given their victories were often small and infrequent, who can blame them when the very bodies holding them to account were falling short themselves?

Many clients in prison were interested in the law, and one of their other favourite areas of the law was the Human Rights Act. They absolutely loved it. Some thought it could be used for almost everything and anything and would do their utmost to shoehorn all arguments in and around it. Obviously, they'd prefer a 'JR', but failing that, a bit of Human Rights was more than acceptable.

Sometimes, they'd phone or write to me, and it was always clear that they'd put a lot of thought and consideration into their ideas. Unfortunately, few of their ideas were legally viable. Nonetheless, I was always impressed with their dedicating time to using the Act to achieve a particular means.

Here are a few of their suggestions:

- Prisoners should be entitled to keep a mobile phone to ring home (Article 8: Right to a private/family life);
- Better prison wages (Article 4: Prohibition of slavery);
- Prisoners should be let out on weekends (Article 5: Liberty) and
- What's wrong in calling a screw a 'Nazi Cunt'? (Article 10: Freedom of expression).

I was also always interested to hear how legal terminology and concepts had entered the prison vernacular. For example, if an appeal was won, they'd say, "It was squashed". Furthermore, if I used the correct term "quashed", they'd correct me.

I also quickly learned how many prisoners were knowledgeable about their rights and sometimes 'shared' or 'traded' the legal advice they'd received from a legal representative with other inmates. This was hazardous because the advice was bespoke for that particular client. Sharing legal advice in this way is as unwise as sharing your prescribed medication with a family member. Advice was based upon the offence they'd committed and the law under which they were sentenced. Therefore, advice couldn't automatically be applied in a blanket fashion to other people and shouldn't have been circulated. However, it sometimes was.

Like many firms, we had our regulars, and it's true that when we received a disappointing result, say perhaps from a Parole Board hearing, or they were facing a particularly lengthy delay in being heard by the Board, we shared the client's frustrations. That said, we were delighted when there was a good result because we knew how hard many of them had worked to achieve that outcome. That's certainly not to say we minimised their index offence, i.e., why they were in prison, but victories were few and far between, and so we took them when we could, because some of them had worked diligently to achieve a positive outcome and from a very low starting point.

Reading the files of Prison Law clients, especially those who may be set to spend decades behind bars, ensured that those of us working in that area got to see and read about many of the things that brought them there in the first instance, or matters which certainly contributed to their spending a significant period of their life incarcerated.

They are probably some of the saddest and most heartbreaking files I've ever read. They are some of the children whose parents we probably represented in the Family Law Department twenty years ago when the children were taken into local authority care. Essentially, they were part of a cycle that seemed impossible to break.

To sit with a file that comprises a vast body of current and historical reports from psychiatrists, psychologists, probation, prison officers and the like is engrossing. The dossier details and considers upbringing, life experiences and things one may not have even anticipated.

This means that when a dossier is put together for a parole hearing, whoever is reading it has a really clear understanding of the person they're representing and what the Parole Board will take into account when making their decision, which could be to recommend release or a move to a lower category of prison. No decisions are ever taken lightly by the Board, and the client, along with such people as their probation officer, is questioned at length to ascertain the risk of reoffending and the management of any risk.

So, for example, a report may refer to the fact that somebody was raised in the care system along with their siblings. It may cover how they were a victim of sexual abuse by a close family member. Or how they could have been involved with the criminal justice system from a young age. It could explain how they had come from a criminal family or had been involved with guns and gangs in their youth. Attention would also be paid to an individual's history of drug and alcohol misuse or self-harm.

As well as providing a comprehensive background, the reports would look at conduct in prison, progress made and steps taken by the individual to learn about their offending. Recognising the triggers that may lead to further offending and, crucially, risk factors, along with the impact their offending has had on others, is important, too.

Although it's not always the case, I observed that serious offenders have usually had atrocious childhoods and diabolical adolescent years. So much damage taking place in those formative years explains a lot when you learn how others have impacted their lives.

I also noticed that, as a general rule, Prison Law instructions were more often than not from clients who had committed very serious offences and were serving lengthy custodial sentences. Of course, some clients were not expected to be without their liberty for long, but from what I observed, the 'lifers' and those serving substantial sentences made up a large number of the client base due to the complexities of their issues.

Reading letters from clients who clearly struggled with literacy was always sobering. Being able to read and write is something many of us take for granted, but too many appear to lack this skill in the prison estate. Most clients opted to phone the office. They could buy phone credit and call for legal advice, although I think many used it as an opportunity for a chat because they didn't have anyone else to call, which would explain why some called almost every day.

I visited a lot of prisons, and no two were alike, and this was largely based on their category. Prisons are categorised based on the level of risk posed by the inmates and the security measures required.

Legal matters pertaining to many prisoners are about risk management and risk reduction. I spent a lot of time discussing with them how they could reduce their highrisk score, as this would help them on their road to freedom for certain sentences. When clients were subject to parole hearings, they often would want to demonstrate how they had taken heed of the advice of the probation officers and undertaken the requisite courses (for example, educational or offender-focused work), which they needed to access and complete before their next parole hearing.

The difficulty many prisoners faced was the availability of much-needed courses and learning opportunities because of funding shortfalls. I imagine it's a complex area to sell to the general public when there's a shortage of funds and the public purse has to choose between a new hospital wing or resources for schools, versus money for prisoners who may have committed horrific crimes against some of society's most vulnerable. Some of these courses are very demanding and could require daily attendance for months. There are adapted courses, too, for those with specific learning needs if an individual is unable to cope with the demands of the standard course.

When I started to work with clients in prison, I inherited some files from another trainee who had moved on. They were like something found in the wreckage following a plane crash, except there was no black box to tell me what had happened. When I was trying to assemble some order to them, I read some of the letters my predecessor had written, which read like a 1943 Bakelite broadcast. His language was so archaic. It was like reading a document from a war museum's archives. I dread to think what some of the clients thought when they opened his letters.

Inheriting mess and chaos is stressful for me, and I don't understand how chaos doesn't stress other people out, but it seemingly didn't in his case. This trainee's letters also typified what I dislike so much about how the legal profession has traditionally communicated with clients. Some thought it almost mandatory to invoke verbose and convoluted language and litter the page with words like 'hitherto' and 'henceforth'. Surely, the lawyer's skill is to turn something complicated into something simple and accessible, encouraging inclusivity and not sounding like a ridiculous legal caricature.

One of the first clients I was assigned was unusual. He didn't want to come out of prison because he'd got to quite like it in there; in fact, he bloody loved it. He used to tell me all about his ailments in graphic detail, from his bowel movements and fungal toenails to his skin conditions. He'd tell me how he had many problems: physical, psychological, spiritual and mental. Every communication, be it verbal or written, started and progressed in this manner.

He'd list his many problems in alphabetical order and describe them in graphic detail. Then he'd tell me over and over again how many tablets he took every day and which coloured tablet dealt with which ailment. He'd spent so much time on the healthcare wing he thought he was a doctor and would ask me if there was anything of a medical nature that I'd like to discuss with him.

Although most of my prison visits were to male prisons, some were to female prisons, too. I think the vast majority of the women in prison had been victims of abuse, and some of the stories I heard were tragic and sickening. Many had been involved in the social care system, and countless had mental health problems, while drugs or alcohol had often compounded the reasons why they had found themselves incarcerated. I can't imagine how wretched some of their lives must have been.

The first time I saw a female client in prison, she initially refused to come out of her cell, but she slowly emerged in pyjamas. This lady had wild hair, a manic stare and smelt horrendous. We were placed in a room with nailed-down tables and chairs. She was so unpredictable the prison guards weren't allowed to leave us in a room alone together, and they remained nearby. Every time she lurched towards me, they jumped into action, but I think she was just unsteady on her feet due to medication. She did not kick off; instead, as soon as I produced a bundle of papers to ask her questions, she just stood up and told me that she was guilty.

She arranged herself into a crucifix shape, arms outstretched, feet together and head tilted to one side, muttered something about Jesus, and quietly returned to her cell. I felt desperately sad for her. I don't know what happened after that, as was often the case as a trainee, as my involvement was sometimes limited, but I hope she received help.

I chatted with the prison guard as I was escorted through the labyrinthian building to the exit, and as we talked, I learned a lot about female prisons. One interesting thing I discovered was that same-sex relationships were common in prisons amongst women who didn't previously identify as gay, bisexual or pansexual. It's called becoming 'prison-bent'. They're all in relationships of some sort, and a 'Queen Bee' type of character usually orchestrates all the women. I was even told how a full moon affects the women. I laughed, and she said, "You think I am joking, but I'm not." A full moon often precipitates some riotous nights.

I remember when I came out of the prison, a prisoner was being released and met by many family members and friends outside. They were all jubilant, and the newly released girl was handed a large plastic bottle of strong cider, which seemed to go down a treat. This was unusual because many newly released prisoners had nobody to greet or offer them strong cider upon release first thing in the morning. I saw a fair few walking off to the bus stop alone.

Female prisons are far less oppressive than male prisons, in my experience, and I think it's because a number of male prisons are old and uninviting buildings. I'm not suggesting that female prisons would make it into the top ten UK luxury destinations for a romantic getaway; nonetheless, they are certainly less hostile and intimidating. Male prisons also smell so much stronger too, especially for me. I think it's the sheer volume of testosterone in a confined space. When it comes to prisons, I must say that having a heightened sense of smell hindered my concentration.

Splitting my time between prisons and the office enabled me to have a smaller daily dose of the mayhem of the workplace environment. While I'm not a smoker, I'd often venture outside with the girls when they smoked because I loved their authenticity, and they always made me laugh. As they sat on the rubbish bags, chatting and puffing away, one would rearrange her boobs, another would straighten out a tiny miniskirt, and another would try to cover up a love bite with lots of orange powdery paste. As they chatted, the chat would be raucous, and I'd hear about lives I hadn't lived, experiences I'd never had, and they'd certainly use phrases I hadn't come across.

One of the girls would tell the others about "the pounding" she'd received the previous evening when her bloke came over. Another would be saying she was envious, but it was "jam butty week". Another would explain how her "poundings" weren't what they once were because having children had resulted in her developing a "baggy fanny". Another shared concerns about her fella becoming an "Enoch" while another girl was criticised for not shaving her underarm hair and looking like she had "Rasputin in a headlock". It was routine for at least one of them to have a hangover from Hades, be worried about being pregnant, or perhaps both.

What was exceptional was not the vulgar chat, but the juxtaposition of the different staff from different backgrounds. Outside, there was smoking and bra shuffling in full throttle as the boorish humour and rapturous laughter filled the air. Meanwhile, inside the office, one of the non-smoking girls was a gospel singer and could often be found belting out one of her favourite Sunday songs about Jesus while hammering away on the computer keyboard.

It was a large and busy office. Some of the staff passed through, and I didn't get to know them. Some, especially the secretaries, were brilliant. They'd done the job for years, knew exactly what needed doing and were a massive help to lawyers and those of us who were less experienced or had not undertaken their area of work for long. They may not have had the legal background or the opportunity to acquire one; however, they were extremely capable and knew what was what, and I found them not just funny but also incredibly obliging. I worked with a lovely lady who was known to neutralise some of my language in letters, which I think was probably for the best as I could be rather blunt when delivering bad news, and my own turd polishing left a lot to be desired. Some of my letters returned from dictation almost unrecognisable, but definitely for the better.

Brenda would have periods of interest in different projects throughout my time there; tidiness, good timekeeping and eliminating bad language were recurring themes. This was ironic, given that two of the three weren't her forte. These weren't tongue-in-cheek ventures; she genuinely thought standards needed raising, and she wasn't wrong, but it never occurred to her that she might need to lead by example for the notion to be taken seriously and adopted.

So, when timekeeping was *en vogue*, she'd sometimes stand in reception first thing on a morning, counting people in and ticking them off her list. When bored of that, she placed a signing in/out book near the entrance. When she knew about a repeat offender and appreciated that unnecessarily navigating the stairs with her womb should be avoided, she used her megaphone diplomacy on the loudspeaker. She spewed out a handful of names, demanding they verify their presence when they should have been in and at their desks.

To be fair, some people pushed the boundaries, and I don't know how they dared, given the culture, which lent itself to unvarnished bollockings dispensed by an aubergine-faced Brenda. I worked with somebody who was not only habitually late, but when he did get in, he'd always manage to come in holding a coffee from a well-known coffee shop. Sometimes, he'd peddle a 'dog ate my homework' excuse; other times, he didn't bother.

Maybe it's just me thinking through things too much, but if you're running late, perhaps miss the coffee shop. Or, get the coffee, but don't flaunt it. Or, call me old-fashioned, but get out of bed earlier!

My move to working with clients in prison meant I was now working with somebody I'd heard about before meeting him. Few people in the office wanted to work with Noel, and I soon discovered why, and it wasn't just because having him in a room drastically changed the dynamic for all concerned, I was told.

Noel was a bachelor and didn't appreciate having people around him. He had worked in Prison Law for many years, but had never climbed the greasy pole. However, you'd have thought that he was a departmental head by how he conducted himself. I don't know where he derived his air of grandeur from, although I did later learn that he was an excellent tap dancer and knew a lot about rare coins. If Noel didn't want something discussed or disagreed with it for some unknown reason, he'd control the narrative by saying how he was 'uncomfortable' with the subject matter and instructing those around to change it. This was incredibly effective and exceptionally controlling because it meant that people had to stop what they were talking about or change the subject matter to suit him.

I appreciate that not everybody wanted to be privy to everything discussed in the office because it could get a bit Sodom and Gomorrah, and some subjects could venture into grim places; nonetheless, I found his assuming the position of 'conversation compass' and determining its direction of travel quite objectionable.

Some people were unnerved by Noel's eruptions, and others just considered his flare-ups consistent with his being a giant 'man-baby' who had to be tolerated. Brenda defended the indefensible as far as he was concerned, and any attempt at telling her about him was futile because, although we never knew why, she thought he was marvellous. Brenda would turn thoroughly unpleasant with anybody who complained about Noel, so it was simpler to avoid him and say nothing. Sadly, I couldn't avoid him, so I needed to work out how to manage the situation quickly. I did think about buying a book on numismatics, but I couldn't face it. Besides, I was already masking on an epic scale.

It wasn't unusual to see Noel stand over one of the secretaries, deploying his physicality and ordering her to complete his dictation first and not last, even though his work was at the bottom of the queue and other people's work was more urgent. Or perhaps he'd make some unsolicited cutting or personal remark about somebody's appearance if they'd had the audacity to question something he'd done.

Some members of staff, both admin and lawyers, just categorically refused to work with him because they didn't appreciate his talking to them in disparaging terms, belittling them or being subjected to his overbearing and prescriptive nature. However, those with less confidence or gravitas who had to work with him sought revenge by embarrassing him with the people he was so in awe of. So, if there was a phone call for him, they might say to the caller:

"Can you call back in ten minutes? Noel's gone for a poo."

Or, "Noel can't come to the phone right now. He's applying some cream to his rash."

Or even, "Noel's a bit upset at the minute because he's lost his superhero action toy. He'll ring you back later when he's calmed down."

I don't know if any callers ever said anything to Noel, but the call-takers derived great pleasure from these miniature victories.

Noel was notorious for temper tantrums, outbursts and squaring up to people. Unfortunately, it just became 'accepted'. In particular, I struggled with his difficulty with women, especially strong women, because it was like he hadn't taken note of the century we were in. He couldn't tolerate being challenged in any way, and by being challenged, I mean by being asked a question. If the girls in reception asked him when he'd be back as he left the building so that they could manage his calls, he'd look at them as if the premise of their question was completely unreasonable and then walk off.

No matter what he did or who complained about his conduct and volatility, whether from the office or outside of the organisation, Brenda found a range of fig leaves and ladders to help him out of an array of situations he found himself in.

So, for example, if he'd had a row with a security guard when he was visiting a client in prison, she'd say, "Well, he was acting in the client's best interest." Or when he'd had a blazing stand-up barney with somebody in the office over absolutely nothing, she'd account for his behaviour by explaining that he was a "poor communicator". And that was, quite literally, the end of that. Period.

I'd have thought communication was a pretty important skill to have given the job he was doing.

A legal representative unable to communicate effectively is like a surgeon saying to a patient, "I'm sorry I severed an artery when I was operating on you; I've got shaky hands." Or the interior designer who says, “I know it’s a bit garish, and nothing matches, but I’m colour-blind.” You might as well employ a cleaner with a dust allergy or a roofer afraid of heights. I never did get to the bottom of *why* she justified his behaviours because I couldn’t see what he ‘brought to the table’. If there was something I was unaware of, had anybody stopped to think about the collateral damage?

Noel was stress tested daily by the printer he struggled to operate, the fax machine that wouldn’t obey his orders or the mouse that seemed to defy him; perhaps it was a female mouse.

Listening to Noel dictate letters was like sitting beside a human metronome in a low setting. As he became increasingly frustrated and on the brink of losing it, he often kept having to start again. I wanted to suggest that he write the letter himself as it was only a few lines long and would have been much quicker; however, having the impudence to suggest such would have been considered a grave impertinence by an incredulous Noel. Besides, he wouldn’t have taken kindly to anybody offering advice, least of all a woman.

Liberation from Noel could be found by listening to classical music. Having ADHD necessitates peace and quiet at the best of times, and even then, there’s no guarantee that the environment will be conducive and productive for work. Concentration is at a premium and often short-lived, so one needs to seize upon it when afforded a breather from the ADHD.

Classical music became my saviour because it recalibrated my immediate environment by creating an audio ‘virtual reality’ for my ears. I could still see the chaos, but I could no longer hear it, and my ears were grateful. Music with English words was unhelpful because I found myself singing along to it. Classical music was ideal because it could be soothing and uplifting. It regulated what was fed into my ears, which affected how I felt because what I couldn’t hear couldn’t dismay me. Initially, I found it a strange sensation to have one of my senses hijacked from a familiar environment, but it proved invaluable.

I recall one occasion when all sorts were kicking off, and the day was especially chaotic. The phones were ringing relentlessly, clients’ calls were unyielding, the loudspeaker was persistently bellowing every two minutes, and Noel was amid rolling tantrums, having refused offers of help with whatever was upsetting him that day. I had my headphones on, listening to classical music and was reading at my desk. I needed to escape from the mayhem, and watching Noel on the verge of launching the printer across the room because it had run out of paper and he didn't know how to refill it, was like watching someone get tangled in barbed wire. I momentarily looked up to see what could only be described as a silent movie, and the Italian aria I was listening to provided the soundtrack to the scene before me.

The scene was incredibly animated; arms were flung around, there was stomping, heads were scratched, looks were imploring, there was top-of-the-range stress, and Noel was heading for a Grade One listed paddy. The music interpreted the events well, actually, and quite by chance, it was like a running commentary. As if things couldn't get any more surreal, they then did.

As I settled back down to work, I noticed a shadow cast over the doorway, and my razor-sharp sense of smell knew from the pungent odour of poor dental hygiene wafting over that it was Philip, the lawyer who took to hanging around doorways for no apparent reason. I'd reached a point where I just ignored his loitering like everybody else did. However, it was too late to say anything, even if I had wanted to. Linda exited the room like a determined bailiff on a mission to repossess a flatscreen TV and sent him ricocheting into the next room. Given her not inconsiderable size, his tiny frame and bad leg, it's a wonder she didn't cause him some real damage, given how she negotiated her way around the building. She promptly pulled him to his feet without further ado and carried on about her business, having straightened out her vest, like nothing had happened.

One of the clients whose behaviour necessitated regular prison visits was Pauline. To put it mildly, she was quite naughty and could sometimes be absolute dynamite. She was regularly in trouble with the prison. I think it's fair to say she didn't always capitalise on opportunities to develop constructive relations with staff during her stays with them, or 'residentials' as she liked to call them.

On one occasion I saw her, she was alleged to have used every swear word in the swear book towards wing staff. This resulted in the prison bringing sanctions against her. It transpired (according to Pauline) that she'd only used *some* of the swear words she'd been accused of, which were in a totally different order to those reported. This was particularly important to her. Having cleared that unfortunate misunderstanding up, she asked me if she could perform the latest 'tune' she'd written. I've never been privy to such a personal performance, so I agreed to a rendition. I don't know what genre it was, but it sounded contemporary. I sat and listened as she performed her beatboxing while marching on the spot, holding an imaginary microphone and persistently pointing at me. The particular piece performed for me was off her new album, and she hoped to release a compilation upon her release from custody. I saw MC Pauline several times, and it was impossible not to like her because she didn't serve her prison time in the usual fashion. For the most part, she had a zest for life many people on the outside didn't have, which often manifested in being naughty and giving as good as she got.

Disciplinary matters in prisons consumed a fair bit of our time and usually took place in the bowels of the prison. An adjudication is a hearing in the prison which happens when the prisoner has been accused of breaking the rules. The adjudication hearings can be before the prison governor or a district judge, and this was determined by how serious the matter was.

The hearing usually occurs in the Segregation Unit or 'down the block', as it's often called. The 'Seg' is a type of 'prison within the prison' and houses some of the most problematic inmates for varying periods of time, depending upon such things as risks and behaviours.

My first adjudication was in a male prison and was genuinely daunting. This was not because it was in prison, but because I hadn't been afforded any opportunity to prepare, which was (and still is) incredibly stressful because my life is based on routine, practice and repetition. It's vital.

I was sent to observe the process with an experienced lawyer who would show me the ropes, but perhaps, predictably, it didn't go to plan. The person deputed to undertake the advocacy at the hearing was suddenly unable to because he'd accidentally left an old and deactivated SIM card in his jacket pocket when he'd recently switched phones. Within no time, he was required to assist the police with their enquiries once it had become apparent to security guards during their screening process.

It was a genuine accident on his behalf. Nevertheless, I was on my own and unprepared, even by a 'normal's' standard. I couldn't formulate my thoughts personally or professionally and was just expected to do the adjudication, which is the antithesis of how I operate. However, due to the seriousness of the matter with which I was tasked, the hearing being heard by a judge, and the fact that if I hadn't agreed to do it, the client would have been unrepresented, I agreed. I knew he was withdrawing from drugs and liable to say or do anything, so I reluctantly grasped the nettle. I wouldn't agree to this nowadays, but hindsight is a wonderful thing.

As I'm sure you've gathered, I'm not an *ad hoc*, spontaneous or impromptu kind of person. I need to plan and prepare to manage my expectations and the work. Compared to neurotypicals, I process information at a different rate and in a different way because my brain is wired differently, so preparation time is essential. Furthermore, not being afforded the requisite time doesn't serve my anxiety management at all positively.

Having to defend an inmate's possession of contraband is problematic because the number of defences is extremely limited. However, this was especially tricky for me because not only had I never undertaken an adjudication before, I'd had no time to prepare, and this resulted in my not being as good as I could have been, and I found that difficult to come to terms with. Like many autistics, striving for perfection is part of everyday life and falling short of a job well done can demolish confidence.

Segs are not pleasant places, and when I first visited one, the environment and its very essence reminded me of Dante's *Inferno* because it was wretched and hopeless, and it was what you might imagine hell to be like. What's more, I found it all-consuming, and the utter despair on the inmates' faces was palpable, even for me as someone who struggles with reading facial expressions. Some prisoners wouldn't have looked out of place in Munch's *The Scream* because their angst and dismay were so real. It was downright dismal and dire.

I was subjected to an absolute sensory incursion when I entered the Seg. There was an onslaught of noise consisting of wall-to-wall shouting, yelling, bellowing, buzzers, general mayhem, plus the inescapable testosterone stink. Inmates shouted at other inmates in different cells, some threatened one another, and some tried to conduct normal conversations about everyday matters. Some inmates were unwell and in pain, and this was causing them considerable distress. I understand that coming off hard drugs can cause intense physical pain, and I suspect that's what I witnessed.

No prisoners were pottering about. They all remained in their cells and were brought out one by one to go before the judge in a private room. Prisoners were asked several questions, including how they wished to plead, if they'd had enough time to think about what they'd like to say, and if they had any witnesses they'd like to call upon. A wing report written by prison staff was read as were the charges, and then this was where the legal representative became involved.

When I first visited prisons, I thought the security regimes were excessively lengthy, and I wasn't convinced they were proportionate, but I was wrong. I didn't need convincing of the dangers and implications of drugs and weapons on the prison wing, and it wasn't uncommon to see dog handlers walking around with a couple of impatient Spaniels in hot pursuit of illicit substances. However, I underestimated the damage a mobile phone could do in the prison estate. Mobile phones are lethal. With a cheap 'pay as you go' mobile phone, prisoners can conduct criminal activities, orchestrate their criminal enterprises on the outside, arrange attacks on officers, coordinate riots and arrange for the sale of an array of contraband.

Some prisoners treat the trading of mobiles as a business, and with that comes further strife. Contraband promotes 'territories', which promotes a gang culture. High gains come with high risks, and vulnerable prisoners are invariably bullied into 'carrying them' for other inmates.

Mobile phones and SIM cards were the reason for many adjudications we saw, as prisoners found ever more ingenious means of getting them into prison. The risks may have been high. However, so were the gains if successful, and some were prepared to take their chances.

Although mobile phones were high on the reasons for adjudications, they weren't alone. The production of 'hooch' or homemade alcohol was not uncommon. Some brewed it for their consumption, and others to sell or trade. By all accounts, it tasted diabolical, but I guess when you're locked up and either fancy or need something to while away the time, your palate becomes less discerning. It was sometimes called 'toilet wine', because of where it was stored.

I recall discussing hooch with a 'master brewer' once after the matter was adjudicated. As somebody with a heightened sense of taste and smell, coupled with a passion for fine food and wine, I was curious about what hooch tasted like, at least his particular brand. I was reliably informed that it tasted of petrol, but on the plus side, he assured me that while it was strong and an acquired taste, it improved a bit the more you drank.

Inmates were incredibly resourceful in hooch production and managed to deploy various tactics and means when extracting the necessary ingredients out of everyday food to make contraband. I was always dumbfounded at prisoners' ingenuity regarding their ability to brew, especially in light of the limited access to vital ingredients, equipment and significant storage space required, but brew and ferment they did.

When dealing with clients serving lengthy sentences, another part of my role was dealing with their families and loved ones, because life doesn't stop on the outside. With the client's consent, it was possible to explain and share information with them as they were not always able to speak to their relative on the inside, and they'd want to know perhaps how a hearing had gone or when a prison move was likely.

Some of the male clients had particularly complicated domestic arrangements. They may have had a wife, multiple girlfriends, and possibly children to each. So as not to cause a bust-up, it was vital to know who knew what and about whom, as it could become quite intricate, especially because arrangements seemed to change regularly for some.

I developed a system to manage this, consisting of a family tree on the inside cover of each client's file. Some were quite complex and needed regular editing as the family constitution morphed and grew, sometimes in different directions. Some of my family trees were huge and sprawling, like something from an ancient woodland. Many of my trees would have put most genealogy charts in the shade.

One elderly lady, who would regularly phone, sticks in my mind. Her young son had been given a substantial custodial sentence, and by the time he was due to come out, he would be an old man, and she would definitely have passed away. No matter how often I tried explaining to her that he'd only served a few years of the decades ordered by the judge, and he wasn't coming home any time soon, she still called to see when he would be home. She knew he'd done wrong but thought that he'd done a few years, which should suffice.

She'd say on every call how it was time now, and that he'd been there long enough. Except it wasn't time, and he hadn't been there long enough. It was so difficult for her, and I couldn't give her any hope, which was heartbreaking.

If the general smell of prisons wasn't pernicious enough, I don't think I shall ever forget my first dirty protest on the Seg. One minute, everything was going just fine, and inmates were either locked up or talking to their legal representatives and the next minute, all the inmates were banged up, and all of the 'legals' (as legal representatives were called) were shoved into the adjudication room with the judge.

None of us knew what was happening, so we chatted amongst ourselves while the judge shuffled through his papers. One lawyer kept her eye on the door's spyhole and gave us all a running commentary of the events unfolding on the other side of the vaulted door. Before long, our official commentator informed us of how many officers were on the unit wearing all-in-one white forensic suits (yes, white). Some were even accompanied by a couple of police officers with grisly dogs. At one point, an officer entered our safe room and passed through to a room behind us, only to return several minutes later with some big yellow plastic bags.

One of us asked if it was for the poo, and the officer confirmed it was and left.

I learned that day that some prisoners hold dirty protests to compromise health and safety because they know it will achieve a significant and rapid response from the prison. When you feel powerless, you have limited means of creating an impact, and this type of protest will achieve such an outcome. Some clients were utterly frustrated. The same clients would repeatedly ask for help with certain matters, but due to budget limitations and financial cuts, the help they were seeking, for example, with detox, wasn't always forthcoming.

Several inmates on Seg Units had compromised immune systems on account of being HIV positive, and so the prisons will have had to be mindful of their duty of care towards them. Therefore, dirty protests are taken very seriously, not just because they are a clear breach of prison rules and compromise the safety and welfare of others, but also because a prison has legal obligations. After the dogs had been in, an officer went around the cell with a video camera. I dread to think what he captured on there because it won't have been "rust", and there won't have been a "neat little one in the corner" either.

Seemingly, such acts can result in criminal sanctions for the protestor and by the comments coming from other inmates, they were not impressed with "Bobby Sands" as I heard them refer to him. This was either because it meant that they were locked down for much longer than they ordinarily would have been, or their whole day was disrupted. Many prisoners came from chaotic backgrounds, and I noticed they seemed to like having a daily routine and timetable. Nobody told me that directly, but it's something I concluded over time.

When a prisoner was found guilty of being in possession of drugs or illicit substances, they could be given more time to serve in prison before being released to serve the remainder of their determinate sentence in the community. Very few clients felt that being given additional days on their custodial sentence was the answer to a request for help for a drug addiction, and I can see their point. This, of course, increased their time in prison, and while that was the punitive aspect dealt with, the underlying issue of addiction was not, and so the lack of any kind of provision of rehabilitation results in a vicious circle, both in prison and in the community when they're released.

Given that drugs were quite possibly part, if not all, of the reason behind their receiving a custodial sentence in the first instance, nothing was set to change for some. There were people who developed a drug problem only once they'd entered the prison system, which is a testament to how horrific these places must be. Moreover, some weren't even addicted to the hard drugs themselves, but to the synthetic substitutes used to help people come off the illicit substances they acquired in prison.

Inmates who are known users can be subjected to mandatory drug tests, and the lengths some clients will go to in order to pass the tests is remarkable. Not passing the test can result in the withdrawal of privileges, so many need to pass the test, come what may and avoid 'basic' at all costs. Some prisoners would seek to obtain drug-free urine from another inmate and attempt to pass off the sample as their own. Given that they are not just left to their own devices when providing the sample, I heard many an audacious attempt to circumvent the rules.

Some inmates must have bottoms as spacious as a supermarket 'bag for life'. I was shocked when I read what they'd put up there and how much some of them managed to secrete into a confined space. When I fill a bag, I often rummage about looking for something. I wondered if they were the same in that they couldn't always locate what they were looking for. I wondered if, when they ventured up their bottom, they were thinking, "Where did I put my mobile? Was it next to the urine sample or behind the flick knife? Oh no, it's on top of my spare SIM card."

Not a day went by when I could drive home and think the day hadn't been too bad. Without fail, it was frantic and manic every day and all day. From the moment I opened the office on a morning, pulled up the piss-soaked shutters, kicked away a half-eaten kebab off the step and strode over a used needle, to when the answer machine went on last thing, there was nonstop turbulence and turmoil. My drive home wasn't about 'just getting home'. My car became a decompression chamber, and I think without that journey, I'd surely have got 'the bends'.

I was desperate to leave working with prisoners. It was interesting work, and I loved working with the clients, but Noel's conduct was deteriorating fast, and he was nowhere closer to learning how to regulate his emotions and behaviours. Working with him resulted in my anxiety being at an all-time high, and his emotional incontinence was becoming increasingly problematic. What's more, Brenda affording him diplomatic immunity wasn't helping bring about any positive change.

Sometimes, I watched him, and I could see the rages coming on because they were like seasons of the year. There were phases, and one morphed into the next as we progressed through the cycle. I'd learned to read the signs, like a gardener knows it's spring because the daffodils and crocuses come out. Then, when the roses and sunflowers appear, they give away that it's summer, and so on.

So, although I had an idea when we were heading for a tough day, the skill was not to be about when he got so enraged that he almost gave himself a nosebleed. Some days, he could be incandescent by 10 am and then poleaxed by 11 am; other days, it was a slow burn, and then he'd just vaporise. One thing I did learn was to leave him alone pre- and post-tantrums. I didn't even offer him tea when I was making a round as he approached a cusp.

After Brenda had placed a sticking plaster over the morning time-keeping of staff, she moved on to travelling to and from court, which became her next quest. She became sick of everybody drifting to and from the courts at different times and by different means, so she purchased a type of minibus. It was old, orange and rusty, and nobody had been warned; it just arrived one day – chugging, with windows full of travel stickers from different cities around the UK.

As you may imagine, it didn't go down too well with court advocates. I don't think she'd really thought this through because not everybody needed to be there at precisely the same time and they certainly didn't finish at the same time. Still, she thought it was a great idea and was not only pleased with herself, she thought it'd cut down on people going out to lunch after court and perhaps staying out longer than they might otherwise do.

This vehicle was driven by the odd-job man and caretaker Derek, and it could be best described as a cross between a small school bus and what mums with loads of kids have, who also have an agreement with a neighbour to take their kids to school too on alternate weeks. Nobody was impressed, and nobody ascended with glee. It did nothing for street cred. It had curtailed fun, and personal space was at a premium.

They would all pile in and get poured out at the other side. Occasionally, I went to court in it while helping out one of the lawyers. If I wasn't convinced by it when I first got in, I certainly wasn't by the time I got out. The windows steamed up, you could smell who'd had lots of garlic the night before, and as my door wouldn't open properly, I had to get out of somebody else's door.

Derek, on the other hand, bloody loved it. Cruising around, home-made mixed tape of 1980s power ballads playing on the decks, arm out of the window, gentle breeze elevating his comb-over and blowing through his muttonchop sideburns. It got him out of the office and away from Brenda, who was forever on his back. The bus may have meant that everybody got to court and was picked up at the same time, but Derek was certainly taking the longest route to go anywhere, and who could blame him?!

Some clients used to think they'd instructed a personal assistant when they entered prison and not a legal representative. One gentleman who'd received a custodial sentence sent me his bank statements, utility bills and home insurance details and then asked me to cancel them all on his behalf. I wrote back to him, returning his electricity bills and the like, and informed him that these weren't legal issues, so they weren't something we could assist with. Undeterred, he sent them back to me with a letter and told me in no uncertain terms that it'd soon become a legal issue if they didn't get paid and that I should crack on with it, as time was of the essence. This utility bill correspondence went on for some time, with him returning them to me and my returning them to him, explaining once more that this was not an area where we could assist.

Eventually, he became fed up with me and called the office to complain and ask for somebody else. He was told who practised in which area, to which he said, "Practise? I don't want someone who's still having to practise. I want an expert who knows what they're doing."

It was explained to him what the word 'practise' meant in this context, but by then, he thought he was being flannelled and put the phone down. We never heard from him again. I hope he got his gas and electric sorted out by someone who'd graduated from being a novice.

Having clients who were learning disabled, illiterate or had mental health difficulties was challenging enough. Still, challenges were compounded by clients not being able to phone when they wanted to or call into the office. Equally, our inability to visit them without booking an appointment and driving what could sometimes be a considerable distance didn't assist either.

All letters had to be super clear, easy to read and accessible regarding their content, format and message. So, even if one had a client who didn't have additional needs, things were often protracted from the word go. Forms could be posted before the meeting, as we might not see the client for a week or so after the initial enquiry. Even though I need clarity, sometimes I underestimated how others needed it too, and some clients weren't afraid to let me know with colourful language.

On one occasion, a client wanted to instruct us, so I sent him the necessary forms to complete and return to us in a stamped envelope provided. He had to sign them, fill in a few basics and I'd do the rest. There was a section on the form which needed to be completed to say why he should receive public funding. Unfortunately, I had omitted to indicate that I would complete this for him. He filled in all the necessary sections he was expected to do, such as name and date of birth, etc., but in the section I should have told him to leave blank for me to complete, he wrote, "Who do you think I am, Mr hotshot fucking lawyer QC? How the hell do I know why I should get public funding, I just should, dickhead." There was certainly a lesson for me in there when it came to taking the time to explain things properly.

One of my most testing clients in prison was Terry. He was a lifer who was potentially facing spending the rest of his days incarcerated as his violent offending had deemed him such a risk to the public. Terry was also profoundly deaf, learning disabled, had a personality disorder and was a wheelchair user due to being an amputee. A decision had been made to return Terry to the prison estate from a secure hospital, and the move devastated him. He may have been locked up in a hospital, but it was a hospital, not a prison.

In the hospital, there was nicer food, he could engage in education if he wanted to, wheelchair access and modifications were good, and there were nice staff to chat with who understood his conditions. People could sign, and there were decent deaf facilities, too. I think, to an extent, he was institutionalised, but nonetheless, he felt safe and cared for, and life was good for Terry.

When Terry went from hospital to prison, little to no thought had been given to the huge change for him by going from one institution to another. As Terry had been in hospital for quite a while, it must have come as a huge shock, and he struggled to adjust.

I'm somebody who needs and relies upon adjustments, and there are so many people who happen to be convicted criminals who need adjustments too, and either we just don't think about it or, in the case of a prisoner who may have committed some really awful offences, some people just don't care. I think Terry was way down somebody's list of priorities.

While the hospital had been relatively 'luxurious', there was no minicom back in prison, the TVs weren't set up for subtitles, and very few staff knew sign language. I think the feelings of isolation must have been overwhelming for him.

Organising a legal visit with Terry required military-grade planning and an army of people. On every visit, there were four people in the room. There was an advocate to explain things to Terry because he was learning disabled. The advocate broke things down for him so they were accessible and easily digestible. It needed to be simple without being patronising. The advocate was outstanding and relayed my questions or comments to Terry for a meaningful discussion. However, the advocate was also deaf, so he and Terry would sign; therefore, I needed a translator. So, there were four of us. It was less of a meeting and more of a summit. One of the things I found quite difficult at first was ignoring the translator and just listening to the advocate or Terry, even though they were not speaking directly to me. This experience really tested my skills of social interaction.

This and every other meeting were incredibly protracted. In the first instance, my question went via the translator and then to the advocate, who explained and discussed it with Terry. There was a running commentary of this via the translator back to me, and then the final answer was fed back to me via the advocate, via the translator.

Every meeting was exhausting, and what would ordinarily be a one-hour meeting became a three-hour meeting. I also found it difficult as I think it necessitated the ability to pick up on certain unspoken social cues, like knowing when not to speak and who to look at, because the person speaking wasn't necessarily the one who had something to say. I found the dynamics extremely complicated and wasn't sure how to work them out.

The prison was not particularly well equipped to work with someone with Terry's needs. When I first visited him, they brought in a different prisoner with the same name. This poor guy did not know us, and we didn't know him, so we all just looked at one another in total surprise. He was met by what must have looked like a bunch of conference delegates and had no idea what was happening. There were so many of us in the room that he must have thought a forum was underway.

Officers had shouted Terry's full name; however, there was a guy on the wing with the same first and second name, so he assumed the legal visit was for him. Meanwhile, our Terry (who was expecting a legal visit) obviously did not hear his name being called, and nobody went to get him, so it took a long time to locate the right Terry.

The particular difficulty Terry had was that he couldn't understand empathy. He could not envisage how his offences must have been for his victims, and so because he couldn't understand the concept of empathy, he couldn't put himself into another person's shoes. This was especially problematic because if he couldn't undertake offender-focused courses around victim awareness, he would struggle to demonstrate that he had developed insight and the ability to change, having acquired the requisite skills. He'd then be unable to demonstrate that he'd reduced his risk and could be safely released back into society. Terry was by no means unique when it came to securing a place on an essential course, but his circumstances were unusual.

Also, as a lifer, Terry had no release date, and so was, in theory, in danger of what was termed 'being warehoused' indefinitely. I could see how some people did get lost in the prison system and of course, Terry's situation was intensified by the fact that he was learning disabled and deaf, so access to offender-based work and courses wasn't straightforward.

I don't know what happened to Terry long-term, and this was the situation at that time; things may have improved in terms of what is 'reasonable', but his story serves to exemplify how adjustments of so many different kinds are needed in so many different kinds of situations to make life fair and accessible. Regardless of what crimes have been committed or mistakes have been made, or indeed, if no mistakes or crimes have been committed at all, people need adjustments made for their disability.

The next time I met Terry, they brought the right Terry, thankfully. However, something amusing happened. It was quite the opposite of my last experience being locked in the glass security capsule, looking like Marcel Marceau, the French mime artist. As the advocate, translator and I had passed through the prison, the translator and I entered the 'capsule', leaving the advocate to catch up. We thought he had joined us; however, before he had time to 'jump in', the door slid closed, leaving him on the outside and us on the inside.

We were locked in, and he was locked out. My heart sank. I thought we were in for another session of faces being pressed against the glass, coloured gas flares going up and SOS signals; but no, quite the opposite. Communication was far from a problem. The advocate and translator chatted through the hydrogen-bomb-proof glass, signing away quite happily and making arrangements for when and where to meet.

It was brilliant and made me appreciate how those who could sign were certainly at a significant advantage in some situations. For that brief time, I, as the hearing person, was left out and disadvantaged. I was excluded. Not being able to hear wasn't a problem; in fact, the ability to hear would have been useless.

When clients had been in prison for a long time, they often created ideas of what the world would be like for them on the outside. Some had no ideas. Some had reasonable ideas, but others envisaged completely unrealistic lives. They hadn't had the lives they described before they went in, so why they thought they were an option when they were eventually released, I do not know. Some made their futures sound something like a feel-good children's classic film, where characters had exciting and surreal adventures. I'm all for hope, but I think it needs to be realistic.

I recall one client who just couldn't come to terms with his sexuality and wanted to stop being attracted to men, so he decided that when he came out of prison, he'd 'go straight', and by that, I mean date women, not necessarily staying on the right side of the law. He'd get a nice house, a good job, marry a decent woman and have children, but there was a proviso. The woman would need to produce a certificate from her doctor so as to prove that she was disease-free, and then they'd take it from there. I don't think there was anything in any children's fantasy film which was as fanciful and improbable as this.

Towards the end of my time in this seat, I recall driving in very early one summer morning. I stopped at a red light and took in the morning air as my window was down. I knew I had a full day of Noel ahead, and I just needed to get through it.

I had my noise-cancelling headphones at the ready and a pile of work to get through. I'd go out for a vegetarian lunch to avoid any comments about Dave-Downstairs' dog not having been seen for a while. Then, I'd call by Shirley's Shoes to see if she was still harbouring the dried fruit in her window. I felt that I'd covered as many bases as possible.

Suddenly, I heard, "Get the kettle on, fat arse. I'll be there in ten minutes."

Initially, I thought it was the radio from another car as mine wasn't on. But sure enough, from another lane on the road, it was the one and only Brenda, roaring with laughter, loads of people squidged into the car, most of whom were now awake thanks to her vocal megaphone. They looked around, wondering what was happening and then, realising they weren't at the office yet, settled back down to sleep, faces pressed against the window.

As time went on, I was slightly less alarmed by Brenda. It wasn't because her conduct had improved or what she had to say was less shocking. I think I was just resigned to the fact that professionalism and propriety were something I just needed to forget about and get on with surviving each day.

Although I spent a fair bit of time in prisons while I was working in Prison Law, I also spent a lot of time in the office. I spent my time undertaking things like drafting letters, reading documents, seeking advice from barristers and preparing written documents such as written representations for the Parole Board. During these summer months, I saw a very different side to the locality, which I must have missed the previous year.

During the summer, the area near the office took on a sort of carnival vibe, but with the ubiquitous police helicopter, customary patrols and smell of cannabis in the air. It didn't start too early, and the mornings tended to be peaceful, but it was in full swing come lunchtime. Think Rio de Janeiro, but without the glitz and glamour.

Music was being played, which could be heard from some distance away. The BBQs were sparked up and emitted the most incredible smells of all sorts of foods from far-flung places. There also often seemed to be a car engine being revved up for no apparent reason, other than to demonstrate a new piece of kit which had been added to make the revving roar. I was never part of the party, but I liked watching it, although I was told not to watch on more than one occasion, in case we were instructed on a matter which came about due to the merrymaking.

Now and again, a chancer would mount a mini motorbike and cruise around for a bit, taking in the accolades and hollering from those driving cars with huge speakers propped up against the rear window. The speed of those minibikes was astonishing, and they'd zoom up and down until a police patrol car would appear from nowhere, and then what appeared to be a cat-and-mouse scenario ensued, with everyone cheering for the mouse.

Sometimes, I felt like I'd done my own mini-prison sentence being subjected to Noel for all that time, but the pill was sugared because I knew it was time to move on.

Having completed three of my seats, I think I was not only getting the hang of files and the role of a solicitor, but I was also becoming slightly less alarmed by the office environment. I continued to watch my colleagues and how they managed Brenda to see what I could learn. I knew I could never reach their level of proficiency; nonetheless, I watched in awe.

Some shrugged their shoulders. Some knew it was an inevitable consequence of working there. One person I worked with likened the culture to being in a complicated and gruelling personal relationship. This was explained to me in the sense that although it's bad, you hope at some point it'll change, but it never does. So, you either have to accept it or leave. Some, of course, did leave.

I had also seen things which had given me food for thought. I often processed these thoughts during the decompression of the drive home. I'd think not only about the day, but the wider issues. These thoughts would invariably bring me back to disability and how inequitable things were for those of us (and I mean myself and the clients) who couldn't have our 'reasonable adjustments' dealt with by way of a ramp, a lift or level access to a building. This was because the nature of the disability necessitated a whole different mindset. Still, I don't think that 'the memo' has been successfully delivered to enough people, i.e., those people who could really make a difference.

I slowly realised that both I *and* the clients were making adjustments for the 'normals' in society. I also think some of them had given up trying to explain that they didn't understand or they couldn't follow something.

If a client were to have asked to have something printed on coloured paper, this could be made available. Or if, say, they required text in a particular typeface or font size, then this could have been arranged. Or perhaps they needed to have things explained in a certain way; this, too, could be facilitated.

But you don't know what you don't know!

If you don't *know* that this adjustment will make a difference, how do you know it's what you need? I suspect there are huge numbers of people with additional invisible needs, who have never been picked up. I was only identified later in life, due to a career change. If clients cannot genuinely engage in a process, I wonder if they are having a fair hearing or can access justice in a meaningful way.

I was already acutely aware that I had to adjust for the 'normals' because of their shortcomings, but I was also having to make adjustments for my clients, which I hadn't considered.

Were the blind leading the blind?

I don't think so. I was asking these questions, whereas others in the know didn't appear to have given it a second thought.

I had to ensure that information was clear and accessible to clients. I needed to work around the fact that some of them had a learning disability despite not being told this was the case. And there were others whose mental health condition required an entirely different approach than I'd adopted earlier.

I'd seen the state either fail to put adjustments in place for our clients (for example, Terry), or I'd seen how they'd fallen short of what, in my opinion, was 'reasonable'. After all, with the work we undertook, the state was bringing the case against the client, and yet they were behind the curve when it came to disability awareness, in my opinion.

I'm not advocating a 'softer' approach to those who have committed offences. Nor am I suggesting that we undertake a 'fishing expedition' to see how many people we can find who may have an invisible disability. I am, however, saying that I met clients (and, to be honest, colleagues as well) who I believe were undiagnosed with some additional learning need, and I asked myself how nobody else could have thought this or questioned this. I think until there is a greater understanding of invisible disabilities, how does anybody know what is actually 'reasonable' and, therefore, what needs to be put in place?

Since I've been diagnosed, I've routinely been offered more time, say in an exam or assessment. Remarkably, this has been before I have said what I needed. There was just an assumption. Additional exam time may be appropriate, but it's not a one-size-fits-all. What *is* important is to find out what somebody needs, and if they are struggling and you're not aware of any specified 'reasonable adjustments', perhaps try or suggest different things. Moreover, be open-minded to the idea that something small could make a huge difference.

Furthermore, I must challenge the idea that 'normal' or 'usual' is best. So, for example, do exams have to be written? Are there other ways to assess knowledge or ability? Could more be done orally, perhaps? We need to start thinking about assessments (all assessments in all areas) differently, because the best candidates may be precluded from showing their worth and therefore, we're all missing out.

I'm not saying that exams should be abolished, because demonstrating that you have reached a certain level is essential, but does it have to be done via a raft of three-hour written exams? And don't even get me started on multiple choice questions (MCQs), as they're often written in such a way that somebody with autism is likely to find the phrasing very troublesome.

While enduring the marathon of legal exams for my LPC, I worked out what I needed to score on each paper to pass, but taking into account that I had to guess all of the MCQs, I was unlikely to gain many, if any, points from those questions.

So, I ensured that I was very good in all the non-MCQ areas of assessment and that I could pass the exam on the parts I did well on alone, i.e., without any of the MCQs, and if I guessed any of them correctly, then it was a bonus.

A high-risk strategy, I know, but it was my only option, and it worked because I struggle so much with how MCQs are phrased (along with the fact that they usually involve a complicated tax calculation on the LPC); therefore, they were a write-off in any event.

So, were these assessments a success?

They were for me on paper, but I don't think they achieved their assessment aims. Instead, they were just another neurotypical set of rules for which I had to find an atypical solution.

I don't need questions, whether in an exam or everyday life, to be easier; I need them to be *accessible*, and I think many neurodivergent people would concur with this. I need the questions to be clearly set out as my thought process isn't always linear, as ADHD can make my thinking jumbled, and I need to be sure of what is being asked of me. I need to be confident that the language isn't ambiguous or non-specific and that words with multiple meanings are avoided in favour of words more likely to have fewer possible interpretations. It's also helpful if the text isn't all squashed together.

Finally, if there is a period of teaching before a test or exam, I need to have things explained in a logical and coherent format. No mind maps or spider diagrams for me, thank you, because I have a chaotic enough mind as it is. Give me numbered lists or bullet points, which should always be possible. I 'encouraged' some of the most resistant solicitors to provide me with a bullet point 'shopping list', and everything they requested was completed, just as they'd requested.

Clarity and writing things down for those with neurodivergent conditions will go a long way. The autistic person will likely appreciate it because of how we process information. If things are clear, the autistic person is less likely to take things literally or deviate off the M8 motorway and onto a B road, as much in my view, as per my earlier driving analogy.

Somebody with dyslexia or dyscalculia may appreciate this because they could have a poor 'working memory' and not be able to retain the last thing they heard particularly well or in any particular accessible order.

The person with attention difficulties is less likely to be distracted if things are digestible, and even if they are jumbled in their mind, they can return to the text to aid with processing. What's more, I've known 'normals' say how clarity can be really helpful for them, too, so it's not just the neurodivergent you may be helping.

When I had a client struggling to grasp a process or idea, whether I was speaking to them or writing to them, I took time to try and ensure that what was being communicated was as clear, precise, concise and specific as possible. Even if somebody didn't have additional needs, there was no harm done.

These are just some ideas. I can't diagnose conditions even if I suspect them based on my experiences and learning. Through trial and error, I've determined these coping strategies, which are the best ones for me. Therefore, if any of this can help other people, then I'll be delighted.

This may all sound like hard work to some. That said, I urge everyone to see it as an opportunity. Difference can bring benefits due to a different way of thinking and that's no bad thing. If we don't switch how we look at, understand and treat neurodivergent people, nothing will change. Remember, only 29% of autistic adults are employed.

I wasn't sorry to shortly be moving to another seat. I knew I would miss some of the clients because a fair few were lovely to deal with, incredibly polite and grateful for any help I could give them. For some, ringing us was part of their daily routine, and when they'd finished the call, they'd say, "Speak to you tomorrow," and they always did.

However, I was about to move onto what turned out to be my fourth, final and most definitely favourite seat.

Chapter 8
Family

My favourite area of legal practice was care, and by that, I mean Public Law Child Care matters. This is where the local authority, to varying degrees, and in varying respects, seeks involvement in a child's life. This is because they consider that child to have been harmed or be at risk of significant harm. Although we undertook different types of work in the Family Department, for example, divorce and private law cases regarding such things as child contact matters, a fair bit of my time was spent on care cases, and I was absolutely hooked.

Although some care clients had, and indeed were still utilising other departments within the firm's array of services offered, one thing I quickly noticed about care cases was that unlike, say, criminal cases where some may be in prison or perhaps mental health cases where clients may be in hospital, these care clients were just 'out there'.

Some had previously been known to the authorities, but others were new and hadn't been on anybody's radar. Some had almost been living 'off-grid', and it was incredible to think that there were children who had never been known to the local authority before now, especially when the risks and harm they were exposed to became apparent.

Then there were others whose parents, grandparents and even great-grandparents had had social workers. This is not as ridiculous as it sounds when you think how some children could have a nana who was thirty years of age. So, there were whole families, generation after generation, who'd had an involvement with the care system in some way, shape or form, and it was evident.

Many clients were very familiar with the 'language' of the local authority and would often incorporate the terminology into their vocabulary. They'd regularly utilise terms such as 'disguised compliance', 'minimising concerns', 'beyond parental control', 'sustain positive change', 'ability to meet basic needs' or 'compromised parenting'.

Some parents would even communicate this language and these terms with the social worker to counter the local authority's claims. Some also even referred to themselves as 'service users', i.e., in their case, somebody who uses the services of Children's Social Care, as though they didn't question where they fit into the local authority's schematic.

It's not a social worker's job to fix a family, but I couldn't help but wonder why every generation necessitated social care involvement in some families. I suppose I wondered how effective the social worker and their methods must have been if each successive generation required a social worker, but that's what happened with a significant number of people. This, of course, oversimplifies some incredibly ingrained and complex societal issues, but if every generation needs help with their parenting, then something, somewhere, isn't working.

Nonetheless, I quickly learned that family after family were used to having a social worker. Some children even considered having a social worker like others considered having a postman or teacher; it's just how it was, and everybody had one.

Some social workers even featured in children's pictures and drawings when they drew their family, as the social worker was an integral component of the family unit, and they didn't know anything else. I remember one child who'd drawn her social worker in her drawing. He was in the background of the picture and could be seen shouting at her mum, who was crying, and he was writing things down on his clipboard. Not the look Children's Services were seeking to promote, I imagine.

A new department for me brought a new secretary who always made me chuckle with her varying grades of effrontery. If there was a particular lawyer who spoke badly to her, their dictation would go to the bottom of the pile. Her day was regulated by chemicals, namely nicotine, caffeine and sugar. I'd go as far as to say that chemicals largely structured her day. If you needed a letter typing urgently, you'd need to think about which chemical break she was due before you asked where she could slot you in.

So, she'd schedule so many letters and attendance notes before the morning fag break, a few faxes and photocopying between then and lunch, and so on. I'm a huge fan of planning and order, but this was more centred around ensuring she did just enough to guarantee that she didn't have to pick up work from another department. Once she'd done her self-defined 'batch', she'd shuffle into the room of Family lawyers carrying a mountain of files with the letters held in place on the front of the file by an elastic band. She would then open her arms, dump the files wherever they may fall and shout, "Come and get it!" just like a busy working mum calling the kids in for their dinner.

I was quite pleased to be working on care files, because when I arrived in the Family Department, I was in danger of being given the divorce file of the 'Bed Defecator', or the file for a matter where a father had raped a rival ne'er-do-well, to show him who was boss. I'd come across rape cases before, but never as a means of punishment, humiliation and retribution of a peer in that way, for that reason. However, this sadly wasn't the last time I heard of that kind of thing happening.

If you thought that 'Bed Defecator' was rather diplomatic terminology based on the previous pages, you would be correct. He was colloquially known as the 'Bed Shitter' or just 'Shit the Bed', but Brenda was on one of her 'language improvement crusades' the week the matter came in, and so terms of endearment had to be smartened up.

I don't know if 'Shit the Bed' had any other bad habits or if letting rip on his wife's new memory foam mattress was the final straw because I, fortunately, wasn't dealing with the case. Nonetheless, it's a reason and a half for his wife to trade him in for somebody who was a bit more conscientious, or at least has the good grace to pop a *loperamide* capsule at times of heightened risk.

One of the first cases I was asked to go to court on with a barrister was Patience's case. Patience's children no longer lived with her, as the local authority had obtained a Court Order so that they could be involved in making decisions regarding their day-to-day lives and welfare. This could include things like where they lived or went to school. In fact, it could involve pretty much any decision, and the idea is that they will act in the best interest of a child.

The local authority had become involved due to a plethora of serious concerns; nonetheless, Patience wanted to have her children returned to her care. Given how grave the matter was, which had brought about the granting of the Order in favour of the local authority, and why her children no longer lived with her, you'd never have known that Patience was overly concerned.

You knew Patience was on her way into court before she crashed into the hearing because she'd be having a row with the usher outside. She had no volume control and wasn't bothered who heard her. She'd burst in without any concern for her environment, her head held high like it was acceptable to (once again) be super late. Patience proceeded to plonk herself down, chewing pink bubble gum like there was no tomorrow.

I was warned that she'd rock up late for court, and very late she was. However, it was her demeanour, along with her explanations, which stunned me. She bustled into court as though she'd dashed from one hectic business meeting to the next at breakneck speed and boisterously sat down. There was no attempt to slip or creep in quietly, hoping not to be heard.

Patience was a giant of a woman, and her physicality was not to be underestimated. She wore multicoloured clothing, lots of bangles clattered against one another, and huge pendulous earrings jangled around following the slightest of head movements. Given that she didn't shut up even inside the courtroom, this resulted in a constant noise.

"Hiya!" she said, giving me an enormous grin through the dazzling white teeth she'd just had done in Turkey. "Have I missed much?"

Patience appeared to think that she'd missed the first twenty minutes of a film and she could catch up when she'd got herself settled. Then, without waiting for an answer, she dumped a voluminous and seemingly very full handbag onto the bench and proceeded to rummage and ransack her way through the contents. Little to no thought was afforded to the fact that she was in a courtroom and was expected to be on time, courteous and act with propriety. There was no sense of decorum or respect.

It was as though she'd just got to her seat at the cinema and was looking through her bag of sweets for a particular colour or flavour.

By this time, all eyes were fixed on Patience as it was clear that she had done little to ingratiate herself with either her barrister, anyone else's barrister, or the judge, and yet she was still unfazed.

Out came the compact mirror, and a large red lipstick popped up, which she proceeded to whizz round and round her great big mouth while managing to cover all of her lips perfectly without, I might add, losing contact at any point. She then ensured that she hadn't got any lipstick on her new Turkish teeth, checked out her hair from different angles, and then confirmed that she was ready for action with a smile. Patience then realised that her look was incomplete, so she added a quick squirt of perfume for good measure, which went into my mouth and eyes and wasn't sensorially appreciated.

Patience had no idea who anyone was as she had missed all of the introductions; however, she was undeterred and sat there as though we were lucky to have her company. She was composed and good to go.

Slowly but surely, Patience realised that she had attracted the attention of everyone in the room and looked around amazed, as she didn't welcome the incredulous looks that her behaviour had generated. Without a moment to lose, she hunched up her shoulders and bellowed around the room with open palms outstretched, "What? So, I've got childcare issues."

Seemingly, this was supposed to explain a multitude of shortcomings that had ensured that she'd fallen foul of every court etiquette known to even the most consummate judge.

The irony was that Patience didn't have any conventional childcare issues because none of her children were living with her at that time, such were the local authority's concerns for their welfare. That, after all, was why we were all in court: to discuss the future of her children, whose needs, it was felt, she wasn't able to consistently meet. Patience's greatest childcare issue was not having her children in her care, so that's why we were representing her.

It was as though Patience had become so reliant and familiar with the deployment of that particular phrase that she had completely overlooked the idea that it no longer applied to her precise set of circumstances. She wasn't making it easy for herself or us, but it didn't end there.

As we hadn't seen Patience in advance of the hearing, we'd been unable to explain once more how best to conduct herself before the court in order to make a good impression. That said, I'm not sure it would have made a great deal of difference. This wasn't her first rodeo and she knew the score.

Patience spent a great deal of time avoiding the social worker and apparently went to quite considerable lengths to swerve her. Evidently, this involved hiding under the window when she saw her car pull up and pretending that she'd emigrated to Benidorm. But seemingly not today.

Today, in the middle of the court hearing, she wanted to chat. She didn't give a shit that there was a formal process underway, and by hook or by crook, she was going to talk to the social worker, regardless of the barrister she disrupted, who was standing up making representations for his client.

Patience did see her children, so it wasn't as if they were estranged. Nonetheless, the small detail that there was a court hearing taking place did not deter her; indeed, it didn't appear to register. She wasn't going to let anybody tell her that she couldn't use this opportunity for a catch-up. She wanted the social worker to get the kids on a video conference call – on her phone, during the hearing, as in right now. Patience clearly thought this was quite reasonable.

Despite being told this wasn't possible, she insisted it was and reiterated out loud all of the things she wanted to say to her children. This list included blowing kisses and drawing imaginary hearts in the air. She even wanted to know if her son had been reading the *Bible* she claimed to have given him, and if her daughter had been reading the Psalms and parables they would often discuss.

It was relentless. Numerous professionals in court were restless and looking around. As you might imagine, nobody was impressed. Patience was warned that her conduct wasn't appropriate. However, it didn't dissuade her at all.

Tactically, she decided to be quiet for a minute, which she thought would lull everyone into a false sense of security, and then off she went again. The social worker decided to look away so as not to attract any more unwanted attention, but it was futile.

The social worker didn't respond to the questions Patience fired at her, in a 'whisper', which, incidentally, was loud enough to be heard across a field. So, while all this drama was ensuing, the poor barristers continued to try and present their arguments to the court based on their client's instructions.

I was new to this area of law, and I was expected to provide notes and a summary when I returned to the office. It was a legally complex and protracted hearing, which made it even more difficult for me to follow, and so I don't think that I did one of my best jobs of note-taking that day.

Patience didn't take kindly to being ignored and so sought to regain her composure by reapplying her lipstick, although it can't have been necessary, even by the standards of a prisoner's glamorous wife.

Having received her final warning by way of a glare from our barrister (although she didn't know that he was her barrister because she'd missed all of the introductions), Patience petulantly threw herself back in her chair and looked around the room decidedly bored, but this wasn't for long. She rummaged through her bag and took a pen out. Then, without asking, she ripped a piece of paper from my pad (notes and all) and started to write and write and write. Nobody took much notice of this as she was quiet and not bothering anybody, and I initially thought that perhaps she'd seen sense, calmed down and was taking some notes or at least making a list of questions for afterwards. I was wrong.

Within a few minutes, she was trying to pass a note to the social worker along a row of legal representatives, poking and prodding the ones she could reach while saying in her very loud whisper, "Psssssssst…pass it on, will you, babe? Go on, pass it down, that's right." She gestured with her ginormous index finger and long acrylic nails. She didn't even know, or perhaps couldn't remember the social worker's name, and so just wrote '*The Social Worker*' on the folded-over note.

This note became radioactive, and nobody wanted to touch it or have any part in her antics; I'd even go as far as to say that it was more toxic than the lice file. Numerous people whispered back, "Put it away…you cannot do that …not now."

"Whatever…yeah, I know. Just pass it on, will you?" she replied.

I don't know what could be seen from elsewhere in the court, but our counsel was annoyed, to put it mildly, and Patience was now completely indifferent to everybody's incredulity towards her conduct. Luckily for Patience, the hearing ended, and she could leave, which may have saved her from being thrown out.

Afterwards, the social worker spoke with her as she was required to undertake an assessment of Patience. As she hadn't co-operated with Patience in court, Patience was miffed and decidedly quiet during this time, which was rather ironic.

Children's Social Care had been unable to get hold of her for quite a while, so no report had been produced. I was surprised by this and asked Patience if she had a mobile phone. She eventually conceded that she did, but given the catalogue of excuses she produced as to why she couldn't give her number to the social worker, it was clear she didn't want to comply with the assessment, which, after all, had been ordered by the court. Given that Patience wanted the return of her children, one would be forgiven for assuming she'd have jumped at the chance to be in touch.

The social worker was particularly keen to obtain a number because the last time she'd called Patience to set a date to complete an assessment, Patience had tried to do it there and then on the phone while she was late-night shopping and trying on clothes. Previously, Patience had only provided her seven-year-old nephew's mobile phone number, so the social worker was determined to get her own number from her.

You wouldn't believe the lengths she went to so as to not give out her number, and I couldn't work out why. She either couldn't remember her phone number, it wasn't her phone, she'd lost her phone, or the number was about to be changed, so she'd best wait to have the new number, or it was best to email her.

After I qualified as a solicitor, I worked in Legal Services for a local authority, which was the opposite of the work I undertook as a trainee in the Family Department, where our clients were parents of children. My client at the local authority was Children's Social Care and their social workers.

Patience's case typified something I saw a lot in many of the Care cases in both private practice and when working for the local authority. This was an absolute disengagement with services, and this was more common than you may think. I'm aware that many parents don't particularly get on with the social worker they're assigned or perhaps have a dim view of other professionals, such as midwifery, probation or mental health services, whom they feel compelled to work with. However, they've instructed a solicitor to help get their children returned to their care, and yet are not doing what they need to do to get them back.

Their solicitor is likely to be telling them to work with the social worker and other professionals from different agencies because it's how those professionals assess the suitability of the parent along with any possible risk. If professionals can't assess them, they can't express a view to the court, and if the court can't be confident that it's in the child's best interest to be returned home, they're unlikely to sanction the child's return to the parent.

Parents understand that people such as social workers can make a real difference in the outcome they seek, namely the return of their children and getting social workers out of their lives. And yet, all too often, they appeared to place so many obstacles in the way of progress, either by their own conduct or poor compliance. Moreover, it's not like clients don't know what they've got to do and why, because lawyers go to great lengths to explain things and why they're so important.

When it came to care or child contact matters, I was astonished by the lengths some clients went to in order to prolong matters. This was remarkable as they were instructing us to help them, so they had a vested interest in working with agencies and doing what they could to progress the case.

It wasn't uncommon for clients to say, "Long it out, will you?" or, "I'm not in a rush. Take your time." My favourite was, "Make sure you use Second Class stamps, won't you."

I never did understand this rationale, but it wasn't uncommon, and nobody ever really told me why they felt like this. I suppose it's a bit like going to see your doctor and telling them that you'd like to have some blood tests done, but then telling them not to rush back with the results. Then again, you may say that if you were afraid of what the results may reveal, because ignorance can be bliss for some.

Family Law clients differed from clients in prison or those on the locked wards because they could not only phone and email at will, but they could also walk in off the street. As many appeared to have an inordinate amount of time on their hands, it wasn't uncommon for them to do so with some frequency.

It also wasn't unusual to feel bombarded at times. Some could come in several times a week, and it was difficult to manage them and their expectations. Reception didn't want them 'hanging about in reception' and wanted them out of their way. Brenda always insisted that clients were seen, even if they'd only been seen within the last few days; meanwhile, it was impossible to justify charging the time to the file as it just wasn't warranted, and the government body who would meet the costs of these publicly funded legal matters were justified in querying how funds from the public purse were spent.

This meant that time couldn't be charged to the file every time somebody was seen, which resulted in billing targets being more difficult to meet because not all time spent with clients could be charged for.

Different firms have different billing targets, but essentially, it means that an individual has to bill a certain number of units per day, and a unit was made up of six minutes. So, if you have to bill five hours a day, that means you have to charge for fifty units. These need to be authentic, and you may be asked to account for time spent on something, if somebody thought a task could have been completed in perhaps three and not five units.

This may sound callous and cold, but that was the reality of the matter. I don't think clients whose cases were funded by the state realised how tight the margins were and that there was absolutely no 'fat on the bone'. Conversely, we had some privately paying clients, who were all too aware of our hourly rate, and they kept their contact to a minimum. If something is perceived as 'free', it can have less value for some.

Occasionally, I'd return from court to a catalogue of messages. I had one client who would wait for me outside the front of the office and another, Jasmine, who left me lots and lots of handwritten notes. No matter what the matter was and how serious it was (or wasn't), Jasmine's note was littered with the word "Ergent!" I do appreciate that what's central to one person may be peripheral to another, but I can honestly say nothing was ever "ergent".

Every note had a similar theme…

"*RING ME YOU! IT'S ERGENT. THIS IS ALL SINICUL.*"

Jasmine treated everything the social worker said with cynicism and took very little of what she said regarding her concerns for the children seriously. However, what did become "ergent" was the alacrity with which she seemed to breach Court Orders, particularly ones which prevented her from taking her children out of the country. On one occasion, Jasmine was caught trying to board a plane to the Far East with some of her children on board. When stopped and questioned, she just explained it as a "misunderstanding" and a "little mistake", which was then backed up with the explanation that it was only for one day, a sort of day trip.

Although I was in a new department, Brenda was still ingratiating herself in every microfibre of the firm, whether required or not. At that particular time, her area of special interest was staff sickness. It had always been important to her. To be fair, she always made it into work complete with the 'car people' no matter how unwell she felt or how troublesome her womb was. So, I assume there must have been a particularly bad spell of absences, and therefore, it temporarily superseded travel to court, tidiness and bad language.

Brenda transformed into an urban shaman when anybody rang in sick. She really struggled to accept that somebody was unwell or unfit for work. She'd mentally catalogue their symptoms, along with demanding to know how long they'd had it for, how long they thought they'd be off for, if the person had been to the doctors and if they were out last night. She even knew who supported which football team and would check the fixture list on her tangerine wall to see if there'd been a big match the previous evening.

Now, this may be in part acceptable, as she'd probably had several people swinging the lead over the years. However, if all of that interrogation wasn't bad enough when somebody was feeling unwell, what was worse were the remedies she sought to bestow upon the caller.

We always knew somebody had called in sick because she could be heard saying, "Have you tried…I always use…it doesn't taste nice…you can get it from the chemist…it can sting a bit at first…etc."

If you were genuinely ill, Brenda playing Florence Nightingale and suggesting tonics and preparations would have felt more like Dr Crippen was treating you and would not only have added an extra layer of pressure to somebody who probably wasn't at their best, but the level of intrusion and the investigative nature of her questioning was confounding. I can imagine people sometimes came in when they were quite unwell because they couldn't cope with the interrogation.

A phone call I and countless others overheard epitomised this perfectly. Big Janice had called in sick, and all anyone could hear was a frenetic exchange exemplified by the above suggestions, descending from Brenda's room as the door was open. Brenda appeared to be particularly annoyed, and before long, we were all aware of who exactly was suffering from what as Brenda remained as incontinent as ever when it came to the more intimate aspects of an individual's HR file.

Poor old Janice's haemorrhoids were particularly egregious that day, and she couldn't walk easily. However, as Brenda came in every day, come what may, no matter what state her womb was in, she was less than sympathetic when it came to others and their minor ailments as she saw them. Brenda had a phenomenal work ethic and possessed little patience for those who adopted a casual approach to the daily grind.

The next day, when Big Janice returned to work and shared her displeasure with colleagues, it would appear that Brenda had been less than sympathetic towards the plight of Janice's bottom and clearly didn't appreciate having her remedies dismissed. Big Janice was spoken to, and all we could hear was, "Do you want to look up my arsehole?"

I think it did the trick. That said, there was a real danger of there being a race to the bottom (if you'll pardon the pun) when it came to who could be more audacious and given Brenda's insight, I'm not sure she knew this. However, it does appear as though the best way to manage the situation was to be more Brenda, with Brenda. That said, one did, of course, run the risk of having a card bought with you in mind the next time she was out shopping.

One of my clients with a Family Law matter tested my ability to understand non-verbal communication and inference like no other. Lloyd spoke Jamaican Patwah, and although the language is English-based, I found him incredibly difficult to understand. This was in part because he spoke astonishingly quickly, but also because his instructions to me were conveyed only in part via words; the rest was chiefly through actions, demonstrations, mannerisms and a type of role-play. Appointments with Lloyd reminded me of a game of charades where individuals take turns to convey the title of a book or film to others through mime.

Lloyd seldom made appointments; he'd call in and expect to be seen. He was undeterred if he had to wait because it gave him more time to exercise his considerable charms on any female within the vicinity. He flirted shamelessly with the girls at reception, and they couldn't get enough of him. Whenever I came down to meet him, all I could hear from afar were Barbara Windsor-esque cackles of laughter and girly giggling. Lloyd was one slick operator and had only just met one of them, but was completely unfazed and greeted her with, "Want some good lovin'?"

I glared at the recipient of his smooth words, knowing that all of his lothario antics were only going to make it more difficult for me, as I was completely unresponsive to his extraordinary charms and silky banter, and it certainly wasn't going to make my job any easier to take instructions. He asked if the person on reception could see him instead of me, but he was told that wouldn't be possible. It's a good job I don't offend easily.

Lloyd just walking in off the street wasn't good for me as I'd have nothing to tell him for the most part. I'd explain that there was a process and we hadn't reached the next part, but this wasn't really what he wanted to hear. He thought that things should happen more quickly and that I should have more to tell him. Managing Lloyd's expectations was really difficult because he thought that everything should be working to a timetable which *he* thought was reasonable.

I found when some clients first saw a legal representative, they were so relieved to be seeing somebody that without realising it, there was a temptation to pour out everything they had to say, in one go, in no particular order, like it was a huge discharge of anguish, and in this sense, Lloyd was no different.

Of course, it wasn't a therapy session, but it could mean that some appointments, especially the initial one, were drawn out and could be difficult to keep on track. This, of course, was compounded because so much of the work we undertook involved sensitive and deeply personal matters, with people who felt powerless. This was either because they were in prison, on a locked ward, their children were no longer living with them or because there was just so much beyond their control and the state was so entrenched in their lives.

My understanding of Lloyd's rapid speech didn't improve despite the frequency with which I saw him. The more I asked Lloyd to slow down, the more annoyed he became. This culminated in his throwing his hat on the floor in utter frustration and shouting at me, "Hear me now, Momma!" while rattling off what he'd already told me and just as quickly as the first time. I was listening, I was listening intently, but I just couldn't understand him. The more I struggled, the more frustrated he seemed.

My task for one particular occasion was to take a statement from Lloyd on a specific set of points. Having previously taken a statement from him, I knew I was in for an exhausting time. Lloyd specialised in telling me what he thought was relevant, which differed substantially from what I'd asked him, and trying to get him back on track was like slowly and cautiously creeping from one stepping stone to the next while checking your footing as you go along. He didn't like being steered away from what he wanted to say, even though it bore no relevance to what was required by the court, so he'd physically gesture and enthusiastically demonstrate his account.

Therefore, if Lloyd was trying to tell me what a good financial provider he was (which, by the way, was not relevant in terms of what the court had asked for), he'd stand up, empty his pockets, throw his baseball cap onto the floor, stamp on it, then throw a wodge of cash on the table and then sit there in silence, arms folded, disengaged and looking out of the window. I wasn't sure what I could extract from that, but I persevered to little or no avail.

Having told me what a great financial provider he was, I then received an equally impassioned demonstration about how he undertook all of his children's laundry by hand. I then had to watch Lloyd role-play the act of washing clothes, which involved preparing the water in a bowl, adding soap powder, hanging the clothes out to dry, ironing and then folding them.

We went through an entire week's wardrobe of his ever-growing brood of children, item by item. This was then followed by a re-enactment of how he plaited his daughter's hair and cleaned his son's shoes using proper polish. It was all very endearing, and I could see how he clearly loved his children, but none of it was remotely relevant for the court's latest statement. Trying to acknowledge it while asking for different information wasn't appreciated by Lloyd.

As somebody who needs clarity, precision, and to follow a clear agenda, Lloyd wasn't my ideal client, but few were. I'm not suggesting I'd rather not have seen him, as his case was interesting. He was also very likeable, and such situations made me think more about my shortcomings and what I could do to best meet clients' professional needs. Nevertheless, I don't think that anyone really thought about any additional needs I may have. Once again, it was me who was doing the adjusting.

Having achieved very little with Lloyd on that occasion, he left but not without giving his favourite receptionist a large portion of lascivious banter on the way out. But although my 'people tank' was running very low, I knew I was going to have to switch onto reserves very quickly as I was greeted by MC Pauline as Lloyd left. Even though she didn't have an ongoing case with me, she was very angry and wanted to come to vent. This wasn't as unusual for her (or indeed others) as it may sound, as I witnessed several clients do this when they were annoyed or upset about things that hadn't gone as expected at court, whichever court that may be, and would turn up at the office shouting and swearing.

In she strode, and having sacked us, which she did on a regular basis (whether she had a case or not), she commenced a visceral, esoteric rant. She was angry. Angry with the system and angry with life. She treated us to her customary deluge of swearing, threats, shouting and generally making a nuisance of herself. Pauline, like many of our clients, was ravaged by her lot in life, along with the 'toxic trio' of mental illness, substance misuse and domestic abuse. She bore the battle scars of somebody who was not ready for the life she'd been given and took a sledgehammer to everything in her path, good or bad. On that occasion, the carnage was quite terrifying.

Brenda was called, and she managed to extricate her from the building with skill and a surprising amount of sensitivity. The most remarkable part was that another regular client, Chantelle, had fallen asleep across a row of chairs in the waiting area while waiting for her appointment and had managed to sleep through the entire episode. I wish I could sleep like that.

Having left the office, Pauline pitched up outside, verbally abusing everybody who came in or out while recording the entire process on her mobile phone, and confidently advising all participants in her film that she would be putting it onto social media later.

Brenda was now functioning on a particularly short fuse after the MC Pauline incident, and it perhaps wasn't the best time to go and see her; nonetheless, Philip, who liked to hang around door entrances, thought it an opportune time to venture in. I couldn't think of anything important enough to necessitate a conversation at that point, but I hoped that it was worthy of disturbing her, because she was simmering just below boiling point. I would probably have left it for a while, because predictably, she didn't share his sense of urgency.

Brenda spoke to him abysmally and with a similar level of contempt that many people have for those belonging to a 'flat earth' forum. So, having mustered up the courage to go in, he must have regretted knocking on her door and wished he'd just remained hovering outside.

Just as soon as Philip had managed to squeeze his way into her office and limped around the floor debris, he started to stammer and twitch his way through a question. Brenda cut him short and brutally told him to "Start at the end and work backwards. I'm busy."

At this point, he'd attempt to sit down to make it easier on himself, only to be told not to make himself comfortable because he wouldn't be staying long. It certainly made for uncomfortable viewing because I knew how much effort and courage he'd taken to see her. I imagined that he'd been planning his speech for some time, only for it to come out jumbled and incoherent through nerves and anticipating her intolerance of him.

I could also increasingly appreciate how it was perfectly feasible for somebody to utilise most, if not all, of the firm's departments at some point in their lifecycle, because many of their significant life events either necessitated or resulted in a course of legal action.

While some clients would call in or phone most days, despite my having nothing new to tell them, another cohort required the capabilities of a highly trained military reconnaissance team to track them down. They were elusive, seldom returned phone calls and were notoriously difficult to locate. They'd just vanish. There was even one whom I could only catch when she was having her regular blood transfusions, and remember, she instructed us, not the other way around. The machines used for the procedure were really noisy, and talking was optimum when the whizzing and whirring calmed down, which resulted in my having to be there much longer than I ordinarily would.

I knew she'd be at the hospital for long periods of time. I knew she couldn't go anywhere, and I knew if I urgently needed to get a message to her or take instructions, I could find her there. I even got to know the staff on the ward and a bit about the lifestyle changes one must make when one requires regular transfusions. On one occasion, we urgently needed to speak with her, and as she was elusive as ever, I went to see her on the ward, and she agreed I could take a statement from her. She was in a quiet room, and it was definitely far more conducive to concentration than the usual ambience I had to tolerate.

One of the clients infamous for her elusiveness was Rose, who never answered her phone, letters or emails. It would have been easier to secure a private audience with the Pope than half an hour with Rose.

That said, although she stressed me out as we seldom had instructions from her and were lucky if we could catch five minutes at the court door, she was incredibly likeable and always made me laugh.

Rose belonged to the Traveller community. However, it wasn't because she was away travelling that she didn't attend her appointments. She lived in a flat not far away from the office. I never found out why she was difficult to locate because she never told me. Nonetheless, she never fabricated nonsense excuses either, and I appreciated that because some clients came up with some of the most extraordinary and dubious explanations as to why they hadn't been in touch. I wanted to remind them that we were both on the same side, but I just became resigned to the fact I was dealing with some people who lead chaotic lives, and this is how it was for some.

Rose was entertaining and spirited. Ordinarily, I'd have done anything to encourage that, but not in a courtroom when we were discussing her children's future. Like all too many of our clients, she'd had an unenviable upbringing, and although intelligent, she either hadn't had the opportunity, support or desire to develop. If I could have glued her to the chair in court, I would have and although a poker prod wouldn't have been permitted, I can see how it could have had its uses.

Her case was complicated and multifaceted, and because the number of children she had was approaching double digits, it took much longer than it ordinarily would for her case to be heard. Joe, the father of some of the children, was always in court. He seemed like a dream to handle compared to Rose (in fact, everyone else's clients always seemed like a dream to me). He knew what to say and what not to say. He knew how to conduct himself, when to be quiet and speak when spoken to. In contrast, Rose didn't, and her authenticity didn't help her one bit.

Rose was habitually told, not just by us, but by everyone, not to start on Joe in court, but she did anyway despite them having to sit on different rows in the courtroom like two kids in school who just can't be placed together. Joe had been told not to engage with Rose, and he did his best not to, but it can't have been easy for him.

The hearing followed the usual pattern for them.

Rose would begin by saying his name in a gentle, soft tone of voice. "Joe? Joe?" He wouldn't react, knowing he'd been told not to, so she'd try again. "Joe? Joe? Can you hear me, babe?"

Lulled into a false sense of security by Rose's sweet vibes, Joe would turn around, only to be greeted by a growling and roaring Rose shouting, "I'm going to rip your fucking head off." He fell for it every time, and many of the attendees directed their frustration at him for causing the commotion because he should have known better.

As it didn't work having Joe on the seat in front, he was moved to being further away along our row as a horizontal challenge was thought to be more problematic for Rose than a vertical one. How wrong we were. Despite having people between her and Joe, she'd push me backwards and forwards so as to get to him, as I was now in her way.

I suppose the amusing part was when the hearing was over, she walked over to him and said, "Any chance of a lift home, Joe?" To my amazement, he happily agreed. It was like nothing had happened, and perhaps to them, nothing had.

I was relieved because the last time I'd given her a lift back from court, she'd chain-smoked all the way, having tampered with my radio station and subjected me to open windows and a force-nine gale. I think Rose's life had been subjected to many periods of inclement weather.

There was a client I had been going to the Family Courts with for a while, and she fascinated me because she arrived with her whole family. This 'unit' spoke and moved around the court en masse like one big collective. We only represented one person, but lots of her family came to court, too, so they needed to be managed as one. They got about in a minibus taxi, and in the office, they were affectionately referred to as the 'Chubsters'.

They couldn't all go into the courtroom, but they'd all rock up in any event, and when I say all of them, I mean just that. Our client seldom came without her mum, her dad, her adult siblings (of which there were many) and sometimes even her cousins, aunties and uncles. She brought the whole family tree, root to branch.

Every member of the 'Chubster' clan averaged six foot plus tall, had a dangerously high BMI and had a foghorn of a voice. When they spoke, you'd think that they were shouting, but they weren't. That's just how they conversed, without any awareness of their surroundings whatsoever.

The court wasn't a small building. Nevertheless, they managed to make it feel small and succeeded in taking over the place by virtue of their physicality, lack of volume control and sheer number. On one occasion, they all (and I mean all) arrived at court in white or light-coloured shell suits. Those at even greater risk of coronary heart disease wore white stretchy tracksuits. You could see them wherever they went because they shuffled around in unison.

I was curious about the sartorial rationale and significance of the white attire. Pragmatically, white wasn't a 'go-to' colour if you were hoping to hide stains and spillages and by the smell of some of them, personal hygiene wasn't high on their agenda. I was informed that the reason was to exemplify camaraderie. The children wore chewing gum white grubby tracksuits and filthy trainers which clearly hadn't seen the inside of a washing machine for some time.

There seemed to be an older woman in charge of the cohort who kept everyone in check with her incredibly loud voice. She handed out the sandwiches and wiped the faces of the children who were also in 'white'. They must have been sitting around most of the day when they went to court, but they weren't bothered; it was like a day out for them, and they seemed to enjoy themselves. They brought magazines and computer games and spoke to other family members on the phone who couldn't make it, although there couldn't have been many more relatives, because most of them must have been in court with us.

As the collective couldn't enter the courtroom, they spent the day walking up and down the court, eating flaky pasties and talking on the phone in loud voices so everybody could hear everything. That said, I couldn't help but admire their solidarity and how they all made themselves available when one of them was in need. They were there for one another, and even though they couldn't do a great deal, I couldn't help but be impressed.

Periodically, I'd be given new files to work on. I was told that the new client was arriving at ten o'clock to provide initial instructions. What I wasn't told was that she was a wheelchair user. I think it's fair to say that access to the building wasn't ideal for wheelchair users, and easy access certainly wasn't facilitated by its construction.

What made the matter worse was that as she'd run out of credit on her phone, so she couldn't even phone to alert us. Therefore, she did the next best thing and threw stones up at the window. The more she became frustrated, the larger the stones got until one of them came with the force of a slingshot. I thought that there was a good chance the window had been broken, but it hadn't; the crack was still held together with the tape following a rocket hitting it last Bonfire Night.

As I went down, I bumped into Denise's debt collector, as it was her due day. There were no pleasantries or chat between the two, and it was all very transactional. Denise handed the cash over, and the debt collector lady marked it off in a big book. Virtually nothing was said.

I went outside, and after various failed attempts at trying to get the client into the building, it was clear that it wasn't going to happen.

Sweating and exhausted, I looked in at the shop of Dave-Downstairs and decided that I could really do with a cold drink and a copy of one of his pornographic magazines (most of his magazines were top-shelf) to fan my hot face. So, I passed on the magazine, but I got her and me a can of lemonade and did my best to take some instructions outside.

She wasn't too upset about being outside, actually, as it meant that she could smoke. So, she rolled a few fags, and we had a chat. I could tell that she'd calmed down as the rollup fags became less thin and furiously rolled with the passage of time. It wasn't me who was making adjustments for the 'normals' on this occasion, but it was another example of how common it is for us not to be catered for.

One of the most difficult things I wasn't ready for was breaking bad news, and I had to do more than I'd anticipated when working on care cases. It needed to be done kindly but with enough clout for the message to be taken on board in a meaningful way. Telling a client some of the most basic things, such as that they needed to have a shower, change their clothes or clean the house, wasn't something I had ever had to do before.

However, these basic things were significant by their absence and trying to courteously tell somebody that having a shower isn't for special occasions and throwing a lump of toilet cleaner into the pan doesn't constitute cleaning the bathroom wasn't something I felt prepared for. What's more, when honesty has always taken priority over diplomacy for me, I have to say I really had to choose my words very carefully, and I'm not sure that I always succeeded.

I recall one case which I found very difficult to address with the client. It wasn't because I felt awkward or embarrassed; I just struggled with the diplomacy aspect.

I had attended a meeting with the local authority about a family they had concerns about. The local authority was planning to bring a case to court, and I remember their lawyer relaying what the social worker had discovered and then looking at me as if to wish me luck in addressing all of the problems raised.

Before even getting to the house, the social worker had needed to navigate her way through the garden, which had been churned up by a quadbike that had done loads of doughnuts and looked like it was ready for next year's crop rotation. By all accounts when the front door was opened, there was enough smoke for any God-fearing Catholic to think that a new Pope had been elected. Having fought her way through the layers of smoke hanging in the air, the social worker made her way to the sofa, which, as she sunk deeply into the cushion, emitted the most overwhelming smell of wet dog. It turned out to be dog urine.

Having just about got to grips with the acrid stench, the overspilling ashtrays, the bags of rubbish strewn about and the sticky multicoloured carpet tiles, the social worker explained how she had started to undertake her assessment on 'Dad'. We were presented with the image of a mentally ill, morbidly obese, chronic asthmatic who also had a rotting leg ulcer and was surrounded by breathing apparatus.

Dad was also prone to self-harm. To prevent him from cutting himself, he had had pictures of his favourite TV hosts from over the years tattooed all over his body. Unsurprisingly, he was covered in images of blokes with comb-overs. By all accounts, it worked because he was determined not to wreck his very costly artwork. Dad had declined his old job back at the butcher's as the knives were too tempting, but he was giving serious consideration to a job which had just come up at the takeaway delivering to customers, as he could remain seated and he'd get his dinner thrown in.

As part of the assessment, the family were questioned about all aspects of their everyday lives. This included such things as work/life balance, budgeting, cooking, shopping and the like. The social worker was somewhat surprised to learn that this large and ever-growing family only spent £20 per week on groceries until it later transpired that they had a takeaway most nights of the week, and the £20 was just for bread and milk, etc. For the most part, they had enough money to do this; however, a day or two before their benefits came in, the takeaway shop would give them food on the tick and await the payment until the benefits had arrived.

Once white, the hearing aid beige bathroom was enough to turn the strongest of stomachs. I think even the most tactful and diplomatically skilled person would have struggled to explain the social worker's concerns kindly, but succinctly. How do you sensitively inform somebody that their house is a disgrace?

There was mould in the fridge, sticky carpets, doors hanging off hinges, holes in walls, dog faeces up the stairs, carrier bags full of dirty nappies, a curtain as a makeshift blanket on a bed that had no bedding on it, and a child who'd had twelve of their adult teeth removed due to dental decay. But remarkably, there was an immaculately cared-for litter of kittens under the stairs, in a beautiful bed with soft fluffy bedding. What shocked me was that the family often knew that the social worker was coming to visit and hadn't even had a quick tidy around. Or worse, perhaps they had.

Tackling these issues with somebody who didn't think there was anything wrong with their way of life, and furthermore, couldn't see why the social worker would have a problem with them raising a child there was difficult, because I had to tell them that what they thought was normal and acceptable was far from it. In fact, it was unfit for a child and potentially harmful.

Whether it was due to the home conditions being really poor, or parents being unable to meet the basic needs of their children, some of the conversations that needed to take place were problematic, as some parents and caregivers really knew no better and were quite taken aback to learn that if things didn't improve and they didn't sustain the improvements, their children wouldn't be living there. That was one really tough conversation.

This was my fourth and final seat. I loved care work and knew it was the area I wanted to work in after I qualified, because I thought I could make a difference.

Slowly but surely, I was getting more adept at walking the tightrope of office politics and personality dynamics, although I was certainly a long way from running a masterclass in how to thrive in this, or indeed any workplace.

I remained exceptionally anxious for much of the time because nothing had changed – except for perhaps me in some respects. I was still fraught with anxiety, but I was beginning to see patterns of how people operated and situations flowed. I became more proficient at knowing when personalities should be avoided or safely approached without requiring an emotional high-vis jacket and hard hat. Once again, it was me who was having to adapt and not the other way around. I was gradually beginning to learn what I needed to consciously do to survive.

That said, I was exhausted. I was having to 'mask' on an epic scale. I couldn't be me, because as unorthodox as the office was, only certain kinds of unorthodox behaviours were seen as being within the 'normal' range.

It was 'normal' for Linda not to return to work if she was having a good time on holiday. It was 'normal' for Brenda to drag her womb around the office, or throw her pencil across the room in a temper. It was 'normal' for Denise to have her debt collector come to her place of work to collect her dues, and it was 'normal' for Noel to have rolling tantrums and sulk if he couldn't work the printer.

But it wasn't 'normal' to be brutally honest, say what you thought, or comment on what really wasn't normal, but had become standard. Masking is like holding your breath when you swim underwater. It serves a short-term purpose, but if you do it for any longer than a short period of time, it's unsustainable and detrimental to your health.

Chapter 9
Hands, not Wands

I have only covered a few areas of law undertaken by the firm, but some great lawyers were practising (no, they weren't novices) in a variety of fields and as a trainee, I could be pretty much utilised anywhere.

I was asked to attend a hearing for a very high-maintenance client during my training. It wasn't because I was especially good at dealing with high-maintenance clients, but because I was good at taking notes in court while the barrister spoke and capturing the essence of the day. The case was set to run for a while, so the lawyer with conduct of the case wanted a handle on things as she could not attend.

While I wasn't thrilled at being wrenched away from my regular work and disrupting my routine, I thought it could be interesting. The idea of escaping lots of 'ergent' notes and emails sold it for me, not that I had any choice in the matter.

I was instructed to meet the client at nine o'clock, and from one minute after nine, there was not a dull moment.

As I sat outside the court, I saw two fantastically camp men frolicking their way towards me. One wore an acid green shirt with a frilly front and cuffs, and the collar spread out like a 1970s club singer, purple flares, a black sequined waistcoat, winkle pickers, beautifully manicured nails and sunglasses perched on top of his newly bleached permed hair.

Please, God, let that not be the client, I thought, but it was. He looked like he was auditioning for a place in a 1970s tribute band, not attending a hearing hoping to make a good impression with some quite possibly conservative and cautious people.

The other man wore a dark suit with a cravat and looked comparatively low-key. The first man made a beeline for me and screeched, "Hi! I am Nigel. This is my husband, Jeremy. He's a hair and makeup artist!" as he glanced down at my split ends and then over my spotty complexion.

As he unlinked his arm from Jeremy's and placed his hand nonchalantly on his tilted hip, he noticed a couple of girls walk by and snigger.

"What you staring at, you dirty chavs with your thunder thighs and two tonne of makeup? Never seen a couple of poofs before? Go on, fuck off, you filthy bitches!"

Having roared at the girls, who probably weren't expecting quite such a forthright response, he turned to me and smiled sweetly. It wasn't even two minutes past nine, and the drama had already begun.

Nigel asked if we'd be finished by four o'clock, as he wanted to get out as soon as possible, as they were meeting friends for cocktails, and then he had to get home and sort the rabbits out.

I told Nigel that it takes as long as it takes, but by the look on his face, I got the impression it would be finishing on time, as he'd ensure it.

Over the next forty minutes, while we were waiting for the panel members to convene, I was treated to chapter and verse of Nigel's life, up to and including his meeting Jeremy, the glitzy wedding, am-dram, and just before his first nipple piercing debacle.

Eventually, we were called in for a sound check as one of the witnesses was being video-linked, and they needed to get all the levels right. Jeremy and Nigel sat themselves down, arms folded and legs tightly crossed, while managing to brutally dissect the panel members, one by one, piece by savage piece and with diabolical merriment. Their conversation went something like this…

JEREMY: You'd think she'd get her ends sorted, the dirty bitch.

NIGEL: You could do a lovely job of her make-up. A bit of contouring, I think.

JEREMY: [holding his hands up to the heavens] I don't think so, darling. These are hands, not wands! I'm not a bloody magician. Anyway, never mind her, look at the one at the end!

NIGEL: Which one?

JEREMY: HIM! The one with more rings than Liberace. Go on, check him out!

NIGEL: What about the bloke at the other end, the little crusty one with the transistor radio? Fancy that, bringing a radio into a place like this. Would you believe it?!

JEREMY: Is it a radio? I cannot see from here.

NIGEL: Yes, it is! Look at the headphones. They've got orange foam on them. I bet he's done loads of these, you know. Oh yes, he'll know just how dull they can be, and he's thought to himself, I'll just listen to a few 80s classics and the shipping forecast until we're past the first interval. He looks like he'd like a bit of soft rock to me, what with that receding hairline.

JEREMY: Yeah, you're probably right, luv.

It wasn't a transistor radio; the man was deaf, and this large and rather antiquated device was connected to the loop system in court, and he wasn't listening to any 1980s classics. If I could hear them, then everybody else must have heard them too, except perhaps not the deaf bloke as his 'transistor radio headphones' were on the desk, but everybody else would have been privy to their ruthless running commentary, without a doubt.

When Nigel was called to give evidence, you'd have paid good money to see this performance. He was theatrical from start to finish. He flounced up to the stand full of unbridled self-belief, positioned himself snugly in the chair, moved his shades further back onto his head and gave the whole room a big wide smile, which stopped very quickly when he got around to the transistor radio man, who just received a disapproving sideways glance.

Nigel must have thought he was on a daytime TV show which deals with relationship breakdowns and personal problems, but unlike some of our clients, he wasn't. He was in court and did not manage to directly or succinctly answer one question. Each time, he'd go for an enigmatic response. Nigel provided an account that he thought sounded good but invariably had nothing to do with anything being asked. When asked a question he did not like, he'd throw his head into his hands and refer to one of his nervous breakdowns. He had to have been the worst witness I have ever seen, and I've seen a few. On the positive side, he clearly enjoyed himself and revelled in the attention.

At one point, the panel had to decipher some references in the bundle of case papers, and so weren't paying attention to the room as they were muttering amongst themselves. Nigel saw this as an ideal opportunity to mouth across to Jeremy, "How am I doing?" and, "Is my hair okay?" Jeremy provided a gesture which seemed to reassure Nigel. I wish Nigel had asked me.

Nigel thought he was on fire and loved every minute of it. I think he'd have given an encore and autographs if he could have. The hearing ended, Nigel exited stage left, and we had a pre-lunch conference with the barrister. Exhilarated by his performance, Nigel came bounding into the room with Jeremy three paces behind.

"Well, how did I do?" he asked, looking especially pleased with himself. The barrister didn't mince her words and flatly told him how not only had he not managed to answer any questions from either her or the barrister for the other side, he'd shown not one ounce of insight. Undeterred, completely oblivious and thinking he'd put on a show of Las Vegas proportions, Nigel asked, "Okay, okay, so how did I do then?"

The barrister wasn't impressed and left for lunch. Nigel looked completely crestfallen and looked between Jeremy and me in total disbelief.

"Well, I thought you did really well, babe!" piped up Jeremy. "I wouldn't take any notice of her and her shitty hairdo. What does she know?"

I don't know whether Jeremy was trying to comfort him or whether he shared Nigel's optimism and distorted view of reality. Anyway, the case went on for a few days, and the indecorous comments, running commentaries on hairstyles and inability to afford the legal process the gravity it required continued. I remember towards the end of one day, Nigel decided it was time to go, and he got one of his headaches. He gave me all of his crap to take with me and told me to bring it in the next day. Call me "sinicul", but I think they were on their way out for the night – just a feeling.

I was exhausted after a day of drama. Nigel didn't take kindly to my telling him that he couldn't bring his Shih Tzu to court the following day and that people were unlikely to believe that it might be a guide dog. And in any event, he wasn't visually impaired. I was glad to be going home. But it wasn't to end there. As if the day hadn't been surreal enough, I got into the lift, and a big smile greeted me from underneath a wide-brimmed hat. It was none other than MC Pauline.

My heart sank as I had visions of more beatboxing and rapping, none of which I could decipher. I couldn't handle any more people that day; I was all peopled out and desperate to get into my decompression chamber and home. Fortunately, somebody got in the lift a floor later, and I was saved from the risk of a mouth-generated drumbeat. I did wonder if she'd made any more albums, but I didn't ask. Sometimes, I think some of our clients spent more time in court than we did.

Although I quickly had my own fair share of anecdotes, I used to listen to the folklore stories of yesteryear where some would reminisce over who was the best cat burglar, most proficient shoplifter or who could be best likened to a skeleton key because they could get in anywhere. They'd discuss the strengths and weaknesses of each crook and then conclude how thieves just weren't what they used to be.

Sometimes when the girls were having a fag and chat in the yard on a morning or afternoon break, I'd join them for a catch-up (but not on the rubbish bags), as I'd got to know some of them when I'd been working in their department. As we'd talk, I'd tell them about what I'd been doing along with amusing or unusual things which had happened to me since I last saw them.

Some of these girls had been there for a long time and had some of the funniest, saddest, most peculiar and extreme anecdotes to share. They were terrific storytellers and were able to recount their memories with voices, re-enactments and hilarious mannerisms. I doubt I'll do their versions justice, but here are a few of my favourites.

A call was received to the office from a distressed mother who was at a police station. She'd received a call from the police, who'd advised her that her adult learning-disabled son was being held on suspicion of false imprisonment. She immediately attended the police station; however, they wouldn't provide any further details, so she couldn't provide any further details to us, and so a legal representative was deployed to the station.

This young man's mum had taken herself off shopping for a couple of hours, leaving him at home alone. To cut a long story short, it later transpired that the doorbell had rung, and the young man had duly answered it.

Upon opening the door, he found a very small person who was collecting for charity. Without a moment's thought, he snatched him off the front doorstep, bundled him under the stairs and locked the door with no thought for his own safety. Fortunately, the small person had a mobile phone on him and alerted the police, who shortly appeared (no pun intended).

During the interview, the young man was asked why he'd taken that course of action. Everybody was curious to know because it was entirely out of character. Evidently, when he opened the door, he thought he'd been confronted with a goblin and considered it safest for all concerned that he be removed immediately.

I was reliably informed that there was indeed a startling similarity between the aggrieved party and the fabled character. I know I shouldn't have laughed, but the very idea of a little person going about his business, being mistaken for a folklore relic and being stowed away under the stairs did make me laugh, although I never discovered if everyone eventually saw the funny side of it. When I heard this story, I thought how much I'd like to put Jeffrey under the stairs, not forever, just when he'd demolished my desk with crunchy food and cluttered my area with his little suits. I think he was probably around the size of the aggrieved. And if there was room for Noel in there, all the better.

Then, there was another case where a client came in for a divorce. The Decree Nisi had been applied for, but for some reason, the Decree Absolute never was. This meant that the couple weren't actually divorced. The client went off, got on with their life and was never heard from again for quite some time.

Anyhow, having reflected on the 'divorce' and with the passage of time, the couple later rekindled their relationship, got back together and eventually decided that they'd been hasty in seeking a divorce and so decided to remarry. When they went to the registry office, they were asked for a copy of the Decree Absolute to prove that they were divorced, as this was required if they wanted to marry. They didn't recall having received one, but said they'd go home and have a good look. Having turned the house upside down, they couldn't find the Decree Absolute and contacted the office to see what they should do next. After some enquiries, it transpired that there was indeed no Decree Absolute, because it had never been applied for, and they were still married.

Professionally, this was a clanger on steroids. Fortunately, this couple saw the funny side of the situation, but that was more good luck than good management. It could have ended quite differently, given that they'd been living like single people, thinking they were when they were still husband and wife.

And then there was the bodyguard saga when a local ne'er-do-well had been a bit vocal with Brenda, and an even bigger ne'er-do-well got to hear about the matter and was furious.

Now, for all her faults, Brenda was a mature lady who clearly wasn't in the best physical health. She couldn't walk particularly far without wheezing; her womb featured heavily in her daily planning, and even in her orthopaedic clogs, she was still not particularly tall.

Nonetheless, this chancer expressed his views a little too firmly with her, and this didn't go down well in the criminal fraternity as she was extremely well thought of. So, having dealt with the individual concerned, a large and frightening-looking man was deposited outside the office as a statement to all concerned.

Brenda didn't appreciate this grand gesture and show of might, and despite her lack of height, she would regularly trundle outside, telling him to "fuck off". But he wouldn't go, and she became more and more annoyed, which was compounded by all of the staff singing tracks from romantic films and having posters of heartthrobs all around the office. Even some years later, nobody could sing songs from these films because I'm told that she never saw the funny side of it; saying that, it did go on for quite some time.

Chapter 10
Hoi Polloi

Although I went there to train and to put into practice my so-called 'legal book years', I came away with so much more than the title of 'Solicitor'. I got to see a side of life I'd never experienced before, but I did so safe in the knowledge that I could go home on a night despite sometimes feeling hammered by the day and brutalised by the environment. For those I encountered who were battling with their lot in life, they didn't get to leave.

Sometimes, when I pick over the archaeology in my mind and remember my time there, I recall feeling like a visitor. I'm sure some even perceived me as an imposter, especially because of my 'accent'. Some greeted me with open arms, some with incredulity and others with hostility, but that was okay.

What's more, I laughed. I laughed so hard sometimes that my sides ached. I encountered some of the most riotous and comedic characters you could ever wish to meet, whose razor-sharp wit and effortless ability to bring the outlandish to life left me speechless at times. I've laughed at the peculiar situations and circumstances, and I have chortled at the altogether bizarre and incredible.

I love to laugh, but I don't do so easily, because I don't find very much funny, and yet some of the staff and clients made me chuckle even when it was politically incorrect or inappropriate to do so. Everyday life was so raw for so many of them, and yet the humour they derived from adversity was like something I'd never seen before. I feel so lucky to have had the opportunity to see another side of life, and I think I am better for having seen it.

Moreover, I had the opportunity to look through the 'right' end of the telescope. Looking close up, I can confirm that it undoubtedly revealed some of life's vile underbelly and some of the things I read and accounts of what one human can do to another still sicken me to this day.

I saw up close how some people are born into poverty. Some didn't know about life without a social worker. Visiting relatives in prison from a young age was normal for others. A chronic and debilitating mental health condition was a life sentence for a significant number. And there were those for whom crime was an occupation and spending time in prison is as much an occupational hazard as eating too much over Christmas and having to face the consequences on the bathroom scales come the New Year. There were people who could tick the 'all of the above' box, too, and their numbers weren't insubstantial from what I saw.

I worked with some whose lives may have taken a very different course, professionally and personally, if they'd been exposed to different opportunities and experiences. Initially, some of the clients, with their unpredictable behaviour, intemperate language and unorthodox attitudes towards the state and her powers, shocked and even unnerved me at times because this wasn't a life I'd lived. Then again, I also saw many different lives lived in ways with which I wasn't familiar, and I suppose you could say in the time I was there, I also began to appreciate that there's not just one way to live your life.

And then there was Roy.

Who could forget him? There were his titles, his entourage and his lineage. Roy's case remains unsurpassed, in my view. Not because his legal case was particularly unusual; in fact, it was very ordinary. However, *he* was so extraordinary in a world where pretty much everyone was extraordinary.

As I recall, Roy never received a call from 'The Authorities' advising him of his next appointment. Nonetheless, he still considered himself a feudal lord and was last heard of wearing his homemade diadem; sceptre in one hand and orb in the other. He was seldom without his anointing utensils while admiring coins bearing his effigy. I think Roy's story remains the most remarkable client story because he took it so far and was 'just out there'.

But it's also one of the saddest.

And then there was Brenda. Although there was a fist underpinning much of her behaviour, and while her atrocious language and belligerence often upstaged her many good deeds and considerable kindness, I learned over time that she was also capable of tremendous acts of compassion and benevolence.

On one occasion, Brenda had been called to reception to deal with 'an incident'. It wasn't unusual for things to kick off in reception, or for a 'straightener' to take place between two clients having a disagreement.

Once the matter she was dealing with had been resolved, she noticed that a woman was sitting quietly on one of the chairs, gently weeping while clutching a letter. She was a burgeoning middle-aged lady with a wide mouth containing an army of brilliant white teeth, a colourful tea-cosy hat, big feet tucked underneath the chair, and lots of plastic shopping bags surrounding her. Brenda went over to her, sat down, and asked what was wrong. The lady could hardly convey her words through her gulps and gasps interspersed between all of the tears and anguish.

Brenda persevered, and the lady explained that her husband wanted a divorce, but she did not. Angry at her refusal, the man had sent her a cursed letter. If she opened it, she would be cursed for eternity; if she did not, she would die. Having been placed in this invidious position, she was at a loss as to what to do. She had nursed this letter for just as long as she could bear the turmoil, but her anxiety had now reached such a point that she'd come to the conclusion that she had to seek legal advice.

Brenda listened intently to the lady and asked to see the note, which was now crumpled and tear-stained, having been worked in her hands for what must have seemed like an eternity. With great caution and yet with almost relief, the note passed from very nervous, shaking limbs into the hands of someone I knew could be trusted to deal with this situation.

Having read the letter and without further ado, Brenda ripped it into many tiny pieces. The stunned and horrified look on the woman's face was palpable. She stared down, eyes like saucers in disbelief at the tiny fragments of cursed paper that were casually cascading into the confidential waste bag, and at that moment, it was difficult to tell whether she would cry with joy or scream with outrage. Brenda reassured her that was the end of that, and any ill fate would be coming her way and not the lady's, so she should go home, put her feet up and have a nice cup of tea while, in the meantime, she would have a lawyer deal with things.

Now, this to many people would appear to be an indelicate way of dealing with not only a sensitive but also precarious situation; however, for Brenda, dealing with this curse was a small task between sorting out two alpha male stags circling one another in reception, and the next problem which was never far away. Although her methods were usually unorthodox, and her actions (particularly here) may appear trivial or even reductive to some, the relief her deed bestowed upon that lady was tremendous. While I've often felt frustrated and unnerved by Brenda, her tactics and behaviours, there was a side to her that you couldn't help but like.

And 'the girls'. They were what made the place operate. They lubricated every working component of the machine. They were like the 'behind the scenes' people on a film set. Nobody saw them, but without them, nothing worked. I'll share with you my final but favourite story about them.

Like many offices, the office had a 'bookman'. The colloquial name came from the fact that a company employed a person to come and leave numerous books of various kinds on different subjects for staff to peruse. It normally worked because he'd be paid for books bought and remove and replace unsold copies. However, our bookman was different in that he left books and came and collected the same books each week. Week in, week out, the same routine. I was surprised that they didn't sell because some really nice ones were in there, but they didn't appear to shift. I soon discovered why.

A lot of the girls decided to experiment with some new mouth-watering recipes and dishes, taking turns to bring in lunch, or they'd rota it on different days so a few could mix and match dishes and courses. I often commented on their lovely smelling lunches, which I have to say were a marked improvement on the daily fried food with mandatory chips and curry sauce; and yet, despite the sudden surge of exotic gastronomic activity, still no books were ever sold.

One lunchtime, I realised just *why* the bookman's trips had been in vain. The poor bloke had unwittingly done himself out of any sales by depositing the books on top of the photocopier, which, anywhere else, would almost certainly have been fine; however, he had patently not considered the wily ways of this creative crew.

So, it would appear that they'd taken it upon themselves to carefully photocopy pages of interest, cautiously ensuring not to bend any edges. The books were then neatly restacked just as they had been when they'd been deposited. So, when the bookman arrived, they'd nonchalantly let him in and say how there'd been no interest for another week/month. Then, just as soon as he'd left the building, they'd all race to the photocopier at breakneck speed and plan their next feast.

Obviously, this isn't right; nonetheless, I have to admire their ingenuity and even more importantly, I have to say that the "woman who shits like a man" started to shit something altogether less odious after the change of diet, and the toilets no longer needed circumnavigating after the mid-afternoon fag break. I was very grateful to the bookman, especially when he brought in the juice detox and vegetarian book range, as that really did make a massive difference. If only he'd also brought in some basic management and communication skills books, things elsewhere may have improved.

No part of my legal learning could have prepared me for working there. You're taught how to understand the law, write letters, interview clients and draft documents, but you're also taught a lot of things I never used or needed, such as working out Corporation Tax, drafting the particulars of a claim and how to change the name of a company.

You're not taught how to deal with the new client who comes in clutching a notice of Care Proceedings for her latest child fathered by a "lamppost". Or the client who struggles to sign their name because a rival gang member shot off three and a half of their fingers. Or the client who thinks he's fathered children with countless famous girl band members against his will. Or clients who are children and are a mini crime wave in their own right. Or the client who begrudgingly comes to the Family Courts regarding her children and says nothing other than, "Can I go yet? What time can I go? Will it be finished soon? This is ridiculous. I'm fed up now. Why can't I go?"

Nobody prepares you for the client from whom you're taking instructions, and they have one eye looking at you and the other looking for you, and you're not sure which one to focus on. Or the client who 'calls in' wearing a floor-to-ceiling bubble gum pink fur coat with a Dalmatian dog print fur collar, while looking for the right mobile amongst her four phones. Or the client who insists on keeping his huge floppy hat on in the dock, despite being asked to remove it, because it suits his dress and shoes. Or the client who sits eating last night's takeaway for breakfast in reception and washes it down with a swig of cough medicine. Or the client who wears a suit jacket, vest and grubby tracksuit bottoms to court. Or the client who was given a prostitute for his fourteenth birthday. Or the client who'd set fire to buildings having removed all door handles. Or the client who froze their dead cat in the freezer, until they could decide where to bury it.

And where do I even begin with anticipating the client who drinks two bottles of vodka a day and then slurs her way through my dictating her court statement and keeps trying to light a fag in the office?

Or the agitated client who comes to see you before opening because the office is on a different gang member's turf, and if he's spotted, there'll be trouble.

Or the client who sniffs the armpits of her jumper mid-conversation. Or the client who takes you through the differing etiquettes required for dogging, swinging and BDSM.

Or the client who cries throughout the entire appointment and you achieve nothing.

And where do you even start with the entitlement of a paedophile?

I had to deal with them because they access state-funded lawyers, and you can't pick and choose. But it was okay, because I knew how to calculate Capital Gains Tax, explain a restrictive covenant and understand a Substantial Property Transaction, so all was well in the world.

And I certainly wasn't prepared for being told once I'd got into a prison that the drug dog had 'indicated', which meant that my legal prison visit would have to be behind glass as the dog had smelt cannabis on me. Given that cannabis was often in the air near and by the office, I wasn't surprised that it could be smelt on me, but I suppose I wasn't ready to be having a conversation through thick glass. You wouldn't believe how smug that drug dog was throughout all of this; we just stared each other out. I gave him a filthy look and vowed never to give any money to a canine charity again.

Meanwhile, let's not forget, I was still very much coming to terms with and understanding my own diagnoses and how they fitted in with me while, at the same time, being very much part of me. They may have just been given a name and title, but they'd always been there. I needed to establish the optimum means of managing them and how I could explain to other people the best way to get the most out of me and manage my daily anxieties and goals because I had a responsibility to do this.

As my understanding of my conditions developed, along with how they were inextricably entwined in my persona and always had been, I began to appreciate how invisible disabilities, namely neurodivergent ones, were and still are somewhat shrouded in misconceptions. Despite having my smörgåsbord, I didn't know much about it, yet I'd been unknowingly pottering about all these years with it.

We may have made some progress when it comes to society knowing and understanding more, although we still very much have Everest to climb. But as yet, we're still without the boots, tents and sledges, and we'll remain so until society understands more about what life is like for us and what they need to do differently because they need to change their thinking and attitudes towards the neurodivergent.

There are times when somebody who should know better has spoken with breathtaking ignorance about autism, and it leaves me with the impression that they don't actually believe that we need all the Arctic kit anyway. Then there are some who don't understand our need to undertake the mission at all.

"What's the problem?"

"You look normal."

"You're clever."

"You're a solicitor."

"You can do things I can't do."

These are the kind of things I often hear, but this is one expedition which isn't optional. There are so many people out there who are neurodivergent, and many don't even know it yet, me being a case in point. I was diagnosed later in life, and I'm sure I'm not unique in that sense. Suppose society wants to get the best out of people, and the neurodivergent intend to get the best out of society and their lives. In that case, we need to make ourselves understood, and the neurotypicals need to understand that just because we may look 'normal', we're also different to them and need different things sometimes.

For me, one of the biggest things is to be authentic. I need you to listen, understand, and not assume you know how my conditions affect me. I want you to appreciate and grasp what is being said. Please don't impose your own preconceptions. Just accept what's being said and take it at face value.

So, if we say that the carrots can't touch the peas or we need a fan on even when it's cold and we're wearing a jacket, the answer isn't for us to take our coats off or not to make a fuss about different food groups touching one another. Don't question it.

It's just how it is, and it's the 'normals's' job to get over themselves and stop applying their prototype to us and not for us to try and 'sell' the idea to them so they can try and reconcile it in their own mind and then consider if it's okay, or not.

I've had times when I've had to explain why I need something a certain way, and I haven't always been able to provide an explanation to the satisfaction of an authority figure. That shouldn't be the case. We're already on the back foot; we don't need any more hurdles placed in front of us so that a neurotypical can sanction it in their own mind.

Imagine if somebody wasn't able to articulate a rationale for needing something. Would the neurotypicals be unable or unwilling to assist because we haven't done a satisfactory enough job of persuading them that it's important that we have the same desk despite working in a hot desking area? We may not be able to tell you exactly why routine and sameness are so important other than it makes us feel better, but you just need to accept it and stop having to have an explanation before you can understand. It's just one of those things. If a 'normal' likes eating oranges but doesn't like eating olives, they may not be able to say exactly why. It's just how it is.

During my post-diagnosis experience of the workplace, I never asked for any expensive or onerous 'reasonable adjustments'. My primary requests were around things such as sameness, clear communication, not being blinded by sunlight, not having to sit next to someone who ate strong-smelling foods and wearing noise-cancelling headphones without someone thinking I was just listening to 80s classics to pass the time, being allowed to have my fan on rain, hail or shine and asking not to be pressured into attending painful social events that everyone would enjoy other than me. It's about understanding, willingness to learn and accepting difference.

I've experienced some remarkable responses to my requests for 'reasonable adjustments', and I don't think any of my requests have been particularly burdensome or unreasonable. For example, speak clearly and specifically, check I'm okay with what I'm being asked to do, let me make a list and allow me to ask questions. However, you'd think by the comments made by some that I'd gone into a restaurant and tried to order roast swan; they were that discombobulated. I'm never annoyed when people don't understand neurodiversity because I'm happy to explain things, but I do get annoyed when people should know better or just can't be bothered to learn.

What's more, you can't fix us, and many of us don't want to be fixed either.

We're okay as we are, and trying to fix us or creating an environment which forces us to 'mask' all day and every day is unreasonable. This is about as ethical and effective as gay conversion therapy; it just won't work, and the collateral damage will be significant. We don't think it's us who need to change; we'd like to see a shift in societal attitudes.

I've always struggled with empathy. It's not that I don't care; it's just that I struggle to genuinely and authentically understand what it must be like for that person. I've realised that until you're faced with a situation of discrimination, prejudice or misunderstanding yourself, it's very difficult to understand what it's like for another person. However, since I've been diagnosed, I think I understand empathy more because it feels more real, and I can relate to it.

I've frequently heard people use the phrase 'suffer with autism', but it wasn't until I was diagnosed myself and began to understand autism, its manifestations, how things felt and what my particular brand of autism meant for me, that I began to take exception to this statement.

Like so many statements and comments about autism, it's probably well-meaning, but it's so misjudged and unhelpful. I don't feel that I 'suffer' with autism. I've also had autism referred to as my 'disease' or my 'affliction'. It's neither. People 'suffer' from dementia, arthritis, migraines and strokes. These things bring pain and suffering and have no discernible benefits.

I wouldn't say that I 'suffer' from an ability to hyperfocus on detail, the skill to think laterally or the gift of having a visual memory that many would pay good money for. I think one of the biggest things we 'suffer' from are people's uninformed comments and misconstrued ideas.

However, one thing I would say to a neurodivergent person is that if you want to get the most out of colleagues, the workplace, as well as yourself, it's really important to understand what 'reasonable adjustments' you need, i.e., what you need people to do, or what you need putting in place so that you aren't at a substantial disadvantage. The person with the disability must be responsible for explaining what is required. Therefore, the more you understand about your own diagnosis and condition(s), the more you can help yourself and help others to help you.

I'm not saying that a gold sports car wouldn't be nice when it came to getting to work, but it's unlikely to be proportionate. What is reasonable will always centre around the facts of a particular situation.

That is why I said at the beginning that a diagnosis isn't a roadmap. It's unlikely to say what needs to be put in place to help you. You need to do that, so that the more you learn about your condition(s) and how they affect you, the more you can explain what help you need, like the 'shopping list' scenario I outlined previously. This of course may take some time if you're newly diagnosed and unsure of precisely what you need.

I hope that by sharing just some of my experiences, I can offend some neurotypical thought conventions as well as this being some kind of manifesto to challenge unhelpful assumptions, because I think only at that point may I start to help some of those who fight a daily battle just to be heard and understood.

I wouldn't stop having autism if I were to be given a choice. If I could press a button and become 'neurotypical', I don't think I would. I've come to think of autism as something to nurture. That's not to say it's not testing, but I can think differently. I'm methodical. I notice things others miss. I'm honest and reliable, and I can speak dispassionately with my head and not my heart about sensitive issues without becoming upset, which was very useful with some of the work I've been involved in.

Autism and ADHD

Having multiple conditions isn't easy, but I've learned a lot about this odd couple over time.

I have previously likened having ADHD and autism to having a wife and a mistress, and it is in the sense that they're opposed. I have to manage and sometimes almost referee these contradictions and somewhat competing parties every day.

So, for example, I may need to complete a task. Half of my brain is very focused on it and has worked out how I will do it. The autistic half of me is glad that I have an action plan. It feels comforting that I've devised a structured timetable and know I'll have taken care of all the minor details because there'll be a list and contingency plans.

Meanwhile, the anarchic ADHD half of my brain wants to come in, mess it all up, have a party, hold a riot, facilitate civil unrest and then piss off. The ADHD side will be quite happy flitting from one subject to the next, looking for distractions, reminding me that I can do it later, suggesting that I can watch television or open a bottle of wine because that's way more interesting.

There are some good things about ADHD, too. Ideas tend to come to me quickly, I can be creative, and I can often come up with a solution to a problem before the problem has fully left somebody's lips. However, as I'm getting older, I do struggle to manage my mental energy levels because it's like the ADHD never tires, and I'm the old bloke who became a dad much later in life and running around the park after a toddler isn't as easy as it used to be.

Some neurodivergent people don't think that they have a disability, and I think that's fine; others do, and that's fine too. If I look at the symbol of somebody in a wheelchair like we're used to seeing on disabled toilets or in disabled parking bays, then I don't think that I'm disabled either. However, if I look at the legislation, I certainly do think that I have a disability, and as such, I'm entitled to the protections afforded under the law. Whichever view you choose to adopt is a matter for you, but the neurodivergent shouldn't have it imposed. Where possible, an individual should make up their own mind.

I think you can tick or indeed not tick the 'I have a disability' box on a form. I think you can seek to benefit and be helped by the laws in place if you so wish, because it's a matter of personal choice.

I hope one day there'll be less of a 'one-size-fits-all' approach and more of a collaborative and inclusive attitude to recruitment and services for autistic people and people with other invisible disabilities. It's not that unreasonable when you think about it.

Can you imagine a large supermarket chain buying all of their staff uniforms in the same size and stipulating that none of the labels can be cut out, even though labels in clothes can cause autistic people very real sensory discomfort?

That wouldn't take account of different heights, weights or sizes. You wouldn't expect an employee to shrink or grow into a uniform, nor would you think they were being awkward because they couldn't explain why a pair of trousers was too small or wide. After all, you'd accept that we're all different and require difference. Not all disabilities require the same adjustments, and remember, everybody's autism is the same – until it's not, and that's because it never is.

As I've already stated, I do believe that autistic people make an obscene number of adjustments for neurotypicals because we live in *their* world, and we're working off *their* template, and *they* determine how we are expected to act, behave, feel, think and be. As a result, we're making the adjustments for the 'normals' despite struggling in their world where they set the rhythm and tone. It should be the other way around, but as yet, it's not.

I hope after reading this book, neurotypicals will start to appreciate this, and even if they don't admit it to anyone else, I hope that some will concede that they've allowed or expected a neurodivergent person to yield to societal norms and conventions rather than accommodating and appreciating their differences.

What's more, some of these differences can bring a lot to the workplace. My attention to detail and my work ethic have often been praised. I have been specifically asked to undertake certain tasks that necessitated patience and a keen eye for the minutiae.

I know that everybody has their own 'Everest', and you may think mine is autism or being neurodivergent, but it's not. It's two other things. Firstly, it's other people's misunderstandings and preconceived ideas about autism and ADHD, and secondly, it's the woeful interpretation and appreciation of 'reasonable adjustments', especially in the workplace. Remember, only 29% of autistic adults are employed. This number won't increase unless we make changes.

I recall some years ago, while working elsewhere, being supervised by a very experienced solicitor. When she discovered that I was autistic, she said, "Don't worry, I'll never treat you any differently than anyone else." I guess this summed up her ignorance, and to be fair, she wasn't alone.

So, if a solicitor in a management position can't get it right, what hope do others have in the workplace or other settings?

This lady meant well, and she thought I was worried about being singled out and assumed I wanted to fit in. I already knew that I didn't fit in and wasn't seeking to be 'admitted'. All I wanted was a level playing field, which could be brought about by her realising that she *had* to treat me differently through facilitating 'reasonable adjustments' in order to not discriminate against me, but she didn't get it.

While a fair bit of my post-diagnosis experience has been a masterclass in how *not* to treat a person with a disability, I have to say that I have had some amazing people who have just got it. They didn't have specific training; nonetheless, they just listened to me and worked with what I communicated.

In 2019, changes were made to the Blue Badge scheme, which enabled autistic people and people with other invisible disabilities to apply for a badge. If successful, the applicant or their carer would be eligible to park in dedicated areas and be exempt from certain parking restrictions. Although the scheme didn't previously preclude an application from those with an invisible disability, it wasn't initially set up for this group, and hence, the overhaul took place following a consultation process.

The change to the scheme gained quite a lot of traction in the media, resulting in many people I know talking to me about it, asking my opinion on the matter and expressing their own disquiet on the subject.

Once again, I was flabbergasted at some of the views I heard from some very intelligent and well-informed people. These were people who I'd previously believed had a good understanding of discrimination and the Equality Act 2010. This is a piece of legislation which, amongst other things, protects people from discrimination in respect of what are called 'protected characteristics', which includes disability. Very few of the people I spoke with supported the change. Here are some of the things that were said:

"But there won't be enough space for my mum to go shopping if people like you who can walk start using them!"

"Is it really necessary? Where will it all end?"

"Perhaps it will be okay if they're autistic and struggle to walk too."

"Maybe there should be disabled bays for those with mobility issues and autistic bays further away from the doors because walking isn't the problem for them."

Some people just could not get their heads around the fact that disability isn't limited to mobility or physicality, despite it generally having been treated as such since the introduction of the Blue Badge scheme in 1971. I got the impression from some that an individual should only qualify for a badge if they were profoundly physically disabled, in a wheelchair and looked like Professor Stephen Hawking, or had a built-up shoe, walked with a stick and had a severe gait to their walk.

When an individual is assessed for a Blue Badge, the assessment is rigorous, so if an individual is awarded one, everybody should be confident that it's justified and necessary.

Trying to explain that someone with autism may have severe and debilitating anxiety, which may otherwise prohibit their venturing out if they couldn't park near an entrance, was more difficult than I thought.

There are other groups, too. Some people with dyslexia can struggle with orientation and a sense of direction. The difference between left and right can also be a challenge. What's more, a poor 'working memory' may mean that they would really struggle to find where they needed to be (and their way back) if they had to park some distance away. Then there's the parent of a child with additional needs, who is liable to run off if a noise or something unexpected spooks them. There are also people with invisible physical conditions such as the inflammatory bowel condition Crohn's disease. For such sufferers, parking near an entrance can make a massive difference because not being able to access a toilet in a short period of time could result in significant humiliation; again, that person may choose not to leave the house.

I tried to explain to the unconvinced that just because some laws are finally catching up with the daily lived experience of some invisible disabilities, and these changes are long overdue, this doesn't mean that society and governments have made the right decisions in a timely fashion when it comes to supporting disabilities and *particularly* invisible disabilities.

Sadly, while we've been waiting, a lot of people have been subjected to a whole raft of discrimination, which is totally unacceptable. I am also aware that since some 'normal looking people' have successfully applied for a Blue Badge, they have been exposed to unacceptable judgement and unedifying questions from fellow car users, which I don't believe would happen if they were obviously physically disabled.

Prejudice and discrimination can come in so many forms and guises, and I'd say, for the most part, it's not intentional or done with malice. Nonetheless, we're still receiving a raw deal.

We're still the ones often having to make the adjustments, and not enough people really understand what an autistic life is like for us, especially in the workplace. So, while I know this is going to take some time because we're starting from a low base, please think about what I've said and be the one to make a difference in the life of a neurodivergent person.

It's over to you now. You either now know a bit more about neurodiversity, or you've heard about it from a different perspective. I've tried to explain my lived experience of my smörgåsbord, how I try to manage it, along with others' treatment and perception of me, and I'm sure of people like me.

Being neurodivergent is like being a Lilliputian in a giant's world. We're not seeking to have everything lowered; just give us a ladder, and we'll take it from there.

-End-

Glossary

Below is a glossary based on my understanding of some conditions in this book. This is not an exhaustive list and cannot be used to diagnose. I am not a clinician, and others may have a different view or experience of the use and meaning of these words. However, they may provide some useful information about certain conditions.

I was diagnosed with them all, apart from dyspraxia, but that's probably because I wasn't tested for it.

ADHD: Attention Deficit Hyperactivity Disorder is a developmental disorder. A person may struggle with time management, organisation, following instructions, concentration, focus, impulsivity and risk-taking. They may be forgetful, agitated, restless and not think before they speak. Sleep can be very problematic, too.

Anxiety: A type of mental health condition. Persistent, relentless and excessive worrying with difficulty controlling these worries. This can have a real impact on daily life, be all-consuming and occupy much of the day. Most of my worries wouldn't cause other people to worry. Sometimes, I have anxiety about nothing at all, and I can't explain why I'm anxious.

Autism: Autistic Spectrum, The Spectrum, Autistic Spectrum Condition. These are all terms you may hear. They all mean autism. Some people prefer one term over another, and there's much debate around the matter in autistic politics.

I believe autism to be a triad of impairments relating to social interaction, social imagination and social communication.

Autism is a developmental disability. An autistic person may struggle to understand how somebody else feels, find it difficult to interact with others, struggle to interpret the body language of others, not understand social cues, struggle with sensory issues like bright lights or certain fabrics, become upset about the unfamiliar, have a need for routine, have repetitive behaviours and special interests, take longer to process information, need time alone because people overload is overwhelming and have meltdowns and/or shutdowns.

Dyscalculia: This learning difficulty is related to numbers and maths. Someone with this diagnosis is likely to struggle with how numbers relate to one another and the sequencing of numbers. There can also be difficulties with working memory, which relates to holding information in the memory for a short time in order to complete a task. This information may become quickly lost or jumbled. Poor understanding can be masked by rote learning. Basic coping mechanisms such as finger counting can be deployed.

Dyslexia: This learning difficulty affects reading and writing, but it also affects how people process the information they see and hear. Organisational skills and concentration can be impacted. Dyslexic people may also struggle with maths and numeracy. There could also be problems with motor coordination and knowing the difference between left and right. A poor working memory is also common.

Dyspraxia: This is a developmental coordination disorder. Fine and gross motor skills are affected. There could be poor balance, poor posture, poor hand-to-eye coordination, clumsiness and a tendency to fall or trip. There can also be compromised manual dexterity and difficulty with getting dressed, e.g., fastening buttons. Some people may struggle to pronounce some words and can repeat themselves. There can be difficulties with the perception of different senses, too. There may also be struggles with sequencing and concentration.

Neurodivergent: Someone who thinks differently. This describes somebody who processes information differently. They could have one or all of the following: autism, ADHD, dyslexia, dyspraxia, dyscalculia or Tourette's Syndrome. These are just some examples.

Neurodiversity: Is the idea that our brains work in many different ways and that we're all diverse in different ways. Different isn't less. It includes those who are typical (i.e. the 'normals'), as well as those of us who are atypical (e.g., people who have autism, ADHD, etc.). Some people would include mental health conditions and acquired brain injuries here too.

Neurotypical: I sometimes refer to them as the 'normals' because they're the majority. They think and process information in the way the majority does. They're 'typical'.

Right Hemispheric Deficit Syndrome: Compromised functioning of the right side of the brain. This impacts upon things like basic arithmetic, social/emotional communication, non-verbal concept forming, visuospatial abilities and attention control.

Acknowledgements

To those who've guided, helped and inspired me, thank you.

Thank you to my proofreaders: B, Julia, Joanne and Sue. Your insight and feedback have been invaluable.

Thank you, Deborah, for helping me to get assessed. I'd have struggled without you.

Thank you, Sonja, for so patiently explaining things again and again. It made a real difference.

Julia and Judith: You two deserve gold medals encrusted with diamonds. You were never too busy to help me with the things I struggled with the most, and you always made time for me. You were patient and more supportive than I could have hoped for, and I'll always be grateful for that. Thank you.

Gary from Bubblecow: Thank you for helping me make this happen.

Reference

Information pertaining to 29% of autistic people being in employment was taken from: Office for National Statistics *(2022) Outcomes for disabled people in the UK: 2021.*

Printed in Great Britain
by Amazon

39921396R00116